KU-299-045

KU-299-045

The Swing Era
1941-1942

EDITOR: George G. Daniels

Staff for THE SWING ERA 1941-1942 EDITOR: Philip W. Payne ADMINISTRATIVE EDITOR: Jeanne LeMonnier ART DIRECTOR: John R. Martinez STAFF WRITERS: David Johnson, Joan S. Reiter, Michèle Wood RESEARCHERS: Lea Guyer, Helen Harman, Joan Nierenberg, Karl F. Reuling, Barbara Richey LAYOUT: Leonard S. Levine COPYREADER: Rachel Tuckerman CONSULTANTS: Dan Sibley (graphics), Joseph Kastner, George T. Simon (editorial)

MANAGING DIRECTOR: Francis M. Scott III

GENERAL MANAGER: Peter L. Hoyt PROMOTION MANAGER: William C. Kiefer
SALES MANAGER: Edmund Schooler BUSINESS MANAGER: Terrance M. Fiore
PRODUCTION MANAGER: John D. Hevner INTERNATIONAL OPERATIONS MANAGER: Charles C. Colt, Jr.
EUROPEAN MANAGER: Robert H. Smith ASIA MANAGER: Beto Yamanouchi

THE SWING ERA is produced in the United States by TIME-LIFE RECORDS in cooperation with CAPITOL RECORDS, INC. David D. Cavanaugh, Executive Producer, Bill Miller, Associate Producer. Editions outside the United States and Canada are produced in cooperation with Electric & Musical Industries, Limited, London, England, or its affiliated companies.

© 1971 TIME INC. ALL RIGHTS RESERVED, MADE IN U.S.A.   LIBRARY OF CONGRESS CATALOGUE CARD NUMBER 79-752211

ON THE COVER: Lindy Hop dancers Stanley Catron and Kaye Popp are doing the swing-out, a maneuver in which the partners will wind up separated by the length of their outstretched arms but still holding hands. Gjon Mili took the picture in 1943.

The Swing Era

Swing as a Way of Life

The Men Who Made the Music:
   The Dorsey Brothers
   Bob Crosby

The Music in This Volume

Discography

1941-1942

TIME-LIFE RECORDS

NEW YORK

Swing as a Way of Life

For a host of people—musicians, ballroom operators, critics, singers, record collectors, bandleaders, arrangers, fan club members, composers, managers, dancers and just plain listeners—swing was more than just the music of the time. Says Ralph J. Gleason, whose account of the Dorsey brothers appears elsewhere in this volume: "It was the whole way of life. At first, when I was in my teens, listening to the Atwater Kent after the lights went out in our house in the little New York suburb of Chappaqua, back in 1933, the names of the bands meant nothing at all. And the ballrooms the music came from were so grand and unreachable that it was all like a movie in which you had only the sound track and you made the movie in your head.

"I knew about Glen Island Casino, that holy place of dance bands on Long Island Sound; a kid I knew in high school, who wore the first black-and-white saddle shoes I ever saw, spent every weekend there to hear Glen Gray. But going to Glen Island meant a car and at least six or seven bucks because it was impossible to think of it as a solo flight.

"Then I went to college, at Columbia, and I discovered to my wonderment that this music was available on phonograph records, some of which could be bought for as little as 35 cents. The phonograph was just beginning to come back after its eclipse by the newfangled radio. To play the records, I had to go up to the room of a musical maniac from Binghamton who was studying pre-med and jazz with equal intensity. For his musical education he had two black boxes of 78 rpm discs and a Magnavox. And so, on discs, I met Bix Beiderbecke and Louis Armstrong and Fletcher Henderson and the Dorsey brothers.

"My musical friend took me downtown to 52nd Street to hear John Kirby, Riley and Farley and Art Tatum, and for the duration of my four years at Columbia I went to bed at 8 p.m., rose at midnight and went downtown to hear music. You could get down from Columbia for a nickel on the subway and you could buy a snub bottle of Piel's for 45 cents at the tiny bar of the Onyx Club or the Famous Door or the 18 Club or at the long oval bar of the Hickory House and, if you had nerves of steel, stay for hours on one beer. Sometimes kindly citizens bought more. Sometimes one could just stand in the corner and not be bothered. I was in a corner in the Onyx listening to Waller the night the whole Basie band walked in and got on the stand. We left the club at 8 a.m. and I went to my morning class in history with music ringing in my ears.

"When I heard that Tommy Dorsey was going to play a Columbia prom I got primed for the event with Scotch and a couple of hours of records. I got to the prom early and I was in ecstasy. On that stage, even at the end of the ballroom, the band looked big, and Red McKenzie was the vocalist. Tommy played *Sweet Lorraine* and Red sang it, as always, waving his arms out of time like a plasterer at work on a wall.

"But what really did it for me that night was the pure, singing sound of Tommy's trombone on the ballads, the swinging sound of the sax section behind it, and then the Dixieland feeling when Tommy would do something like *Jada*.

"I didn't know it then, but that music and all that it implied and led to would be a part of my life from then on. It became an absolute necessity to hear the radio broadcasts of all the bands—Goodman and Miller and the Dorseys and Artie Shaw. But it became even more important to get to see them any time, any place.

←Shown on the preceding two pages is Hollywood's Palladium, the largest of U.S. ballrooms, jam-packed to capacity—6,500 dancers. Far in the rear can be seen the Glenn Miller Band, led by Tex Beneke *(in dark jacket)* who had been a tenor saxist and vocalist with Glenn and who took over the band after Miller's death.

"I worked out ways to beat the tab at the hotels. I learned to slip into the Palm Room at the Commodore, for instance, and sneak behind the band. Freddie Stulce, one of Tommy's saxophonists, would let me sit at the band's table; so would Tommy's vocalist, Jack Leonard. In the last set I could stand somewhere on the side and be transported as Tommy would hold up his finger for 'one more' and Bud Freeman would rock back and forth as he blew tenor choruses and Bunny Berigan or (later) Peewee Erwin would stand up, the trumpet singing out over the trombones and the saxes, and Davey Tough's superficially simple but deeply complex drums building and building over the saxophone riffs. And sometimes, with Tommy looking on, Les Jenkins would take a trombone solo, sweating and straining, his bald head flushing with the exertion.

"It wasn't just the music. It was a way of life."

Swing had many meccas. The sound of the big bands welled up amid the sumptuous elegance of the "biggest pleasure palace in the world," Hollywood's Palladium Ballroom, which had dancing room for 6,500 people and 30 muscular bouncers to keep the dancing orderly. On balconies overlooking the 12,500 square feet of dance floor were two restaurants, three bars and two soft-drink bars. The Harry James band once drew 35,000 customers here in a single week, 8,000 of them on a single night.

New York's Roseland had mirrored walls, a ceiling studded with electric stars and hostesses of notable refinement. It inspired stories by Ring Lardner, Sherwood Anderson, F. Scott Fitzgerald and John O'Hara.

Two suburban New York glamour spots were especially important to the bands. Frank Dailey's Meadowbrook in Cedar Grove, New Jersey, was a cheery place with a large dance floor, tables around the dancing area and a balcony on all sides except over the bandstand. It drew large crowds of college kids, especially at its Saturday matinees.

The Glen Island Casino, recalled by Ralph Gleason, was the "cradle of the name bands." It was a huge, rustic building on a small island in Long Island Sound just off New Rochelle, New York. The ballroom was on the second floor, its high ceiling crossed by heavy beams from which hung the pennants of the major colleges and universities. The room was dimly lit. With the moon shining off the water through the windows and the band alternating swing tunes with ballads of love, Glen Island was a romantic place.

Not romance, but radio, made Meadowbrook and Glen Island major plums for bands. By what were referred to, almost in awe, as "radio remotes," the Casino broadcast 18 shows a week all over the country and Meadowbrook, more than 20. The exposure could make a band overnight. Glen Island helped launch Glen Gray and the Casa Loma Orchestra as well as the Glenn Miller, Charlie Spivak, Hal McIntyre, Woody Herman,

Claude Thornhill and Dorsey Brothers bands. Frank Dailey, a former bandleader who ran the Meadowbrook with his musician brothers, could afford to be picky and insist on bands like those of Tommy and Jimmy Dorsey, Glenn Miller and Harry James. Bands competed to play these spots, played for low wages and lost money on their contracts with these places just to get that magic radio wire.

"We were at the Hurricane in 1943 for six months," Duke Ellington once said, recalling a stint at a New York nightclub, "and lost money. But we were on the air five or six times a week, and when we went back out on the road we could charge five to ten times as much as we could before that." Duke may have been exaggerating slightly, but the value of radio exposure was incontestable.

The bands of Les Brown and Teddy Powell often played in the Log Cabin in Armonk, New York, whose dance room was approached through the Log Cabin store where proprietor Auggie Husser offered jams and homemade pies. The customers included school kids.

In dark and smoke-filled Harlem rooms the whiskey numbed the palate but left the ears sharply tuned to music. The Lenox Club was also called the Breakfast Club because here the breakfast-dance fad began. At Tillie's Chicken Shack composer Walter Donaldson promised Fats Waller a drink every time he played Donaldson's *My Blue Heaven*. He played it 25 times before his fingers went rubbery.

Bare, narrow and deep places

Many of the institutions along 52nd Street, Manhattan's Street of Swing, looked suspiciously like clip joints. Ryan's, the Famous Door, Onyx Club and Kelly's Stables were all bare, narrow, deep places, converted from the ground or first floors of old brownstone homes. But they offered just about everything in swinging jazz. Red McKenzie sang along with Bunny Berigan's trumpet. Art Tatum, Fats Waller and Joe Sullivan demonstrated the inexhaustible possibilities of the piano. Billie Holiday sang the blues as nobody else could. In the narrow closeness of the Famous Door, Count Basie's big band made listeners feel as if they were sitting in the bell of the trumpet.

Hotel ballrooms were of course different. In New York, date met date under the clock at the Biltmore, near Grand Central Station, and went off to the Manhattan Room of the Pennsylvania Hotel to hear Benny Goodman. The more knowing fanciers of bands had already heard him, in person at or by radio from the Urban Room in Chicago's Congress Hotel.

At the Terrace Room of the New Yorker Hotel, Tommy Dorsey's band enjoyed what trumpeter Yank Lawson calls the "built-in air conditioning" of an artificial ice rink which slid beneath the bandstand when not in use.

Nightclubs the size and shape of shoeboxes lined both sides of New York's West 52nd Street in the '30s and '40s when it was the Street of Swing. The faithful wandered among places like the Famous Door, the Onyx Club and Kelly's Stables to hear and compare the music of Count Basie, Bunny Berigan and Bud Freeman.

For good music at lower prices there was the Blue Room of the Hotel Lincoln on Eighth Avenue. The owner, Maria Kramer, paid musicians very little but lavished maternal solicitude on them. If a band she had booked when it was unknown later zoomed to fame—as happened with Artie Shaw and others—that band came back and played a cheap date for her now and then. She knew good music and hers was one of the first white hotels to book black bands.

Important as hotel dates were to bands for money and prestige, their fame among a wider audience depended even more on the sales of their records.

The record industry was a prime disseminator of and fuel source for swing. From small beginnings, the U.S. record industry grew to a $50-million-a-year business in the 1920s, then slumped to 1/20th of that in 1932 under the impact of radio and the Depression. It came back strong with the advent of the 35-cent 78-rpm record, the development of the electric-powered record player and the sudden ubiquity of the jukebox. By 1939 there were 225,000 jukeboxes in the U.S. using 13 million discs a year. Youngsters thronged record stores each week when new shipments arrived, to listen, comment and buy.

Radio stations quickly understood the value of playing recordings of vastly popular music. Whole programs could be built on nothing more than a stack of records and a good talker. The disc jockey became a figure of national importance, ardently wooed by musicians and record manufacturers. Disc jockeys and the boxes helped launch some great bands to fame.

A flood of recordings swelled to meet the demand. Not counting transcriptions, the kind of packaged programming sold to radio stations on 16-inch platters, the industry sold 10 million records in 1933, 33 million in 1938 and 127 million in 1941.

Three big companies dominated the swing and jazz fields but there were a dozen significant smaller outfits. Theoretically, most bands made all their records under the same or very similar names and for only one label at a time. In practice, musicians flitted like butterflies from label to label under various guises. Duke Ellington's manager, Irving Mills, signed an exclusive contract with Victor on behalf of the Duke. Soon records appeared under other labels by bands sounding much like Ellington's but called the Jungle Band, Mills's Ten Blackberries, the Harlem Footwarmers, Joe Turner and His Memphis Men, or the Philadelphia Melodians.

Commodore records issued some fine sides attributed to a musician identified simply as "Maurice" who sounded exactly like Fats Waller.

Shoeless Joe Jackson, the star outfielder who was banned from baseball after being accused of conspiring to throw the 1919 World Series, got his name on some record labels, but the clarinet on those records was Benny Goodman's.

Clef Records had some brilliant drum solos credited to the Chicago Flash, which does in a way describe Gene Krupa.

Bands did some of this label-hopping for extra money, a need which eventually disappeared in cases like Ellington's. But often musicians played under *noms de disque* just for the fun of it. Sidemen from different bands who particularly enjoyed playing together would sometimes combine forces for a recording session, no matter what their contracts said.

During the Swing Era, almost all popular records were ten-inch, 78-rpm discs which gave the musicians about three minutes to play a tune. "That was the good part about it," Earl Hines contends. "Just like when you are on stage, you want to leave the people wanting more. You concentrate more, you're getting to the meat of it because you know you're only going to be there for a certain length of time. When I got only two choruses to play I put everything I've got into them. There was more feeling in doing our recording than there is now."

Hines has his doubts about today's long-playing records. "It is a mistake putting out albums with ten or so tunes on them," he says. "Good tunes get lost that way. The disc jockeys never play the whole album, maybe just one tune they like, and the public never gets to hear the other tunes. Years ago we'd make just one record and it would last three months, and if it would go well they would keep it out there and you got time to see what was happening, you got new ideas."

Despite the advent of the LP—or perhaps because of it—collectors of 78s still abound. Many Swing Era collectors began by buying used jukebox records at ten cents each and graduated to buying every disc by their favorite bands they could lay their hands on. Some became real fanatics who scoured attics, basements and secondhand stores, joined collecting clubs and became part of a vast network of shellac-hoarders.

Collections grew until they threatened to take over whole houses. Alan Merriam, now an ethnomusicologist and a professor at Indiana University, remembers visiting the home of Edwin ("Squirrel") Ashcraft, the Chicago lawyer and early swing fan, at four o'clock one morning and being astonished at the piles of records, some of them great rarities, stacked without jackets in wobbly piles on chairs, tables and the floor. Ashcraft

Shuttle runs of taxis carried white people from downtown Manhattan up to Harlem's fabulous Cotton Club on Lenox Avenue where the delights included the music of the Duke Ellington, Cab Calloway and Jimmie Lunceford bands plus singers and tall, tan chorus girls doing, among other dances, the Harlem River Quiver.

was an untypically generous collector who freely gave away records to friends. Jacob Schneider, a New York collector, was and is more businesslike. He set out to amass the world's largest collection of its kind and believes he has it now—450,000 jazz, pop, sweet and personality records dating from about 1910 to 1955.

Swing fans listened endlessly to records and also spent considerable time dancing—to recorded music when necessary but preferably to the sounds of a live band.

Dancing was the central activity in the hotel and supper clubs, in the ballrooms or at the college proms. Most people danced the fox-trot, a simple shuffle that a spastic could master and a man with a dickey heart

could safely dance all night. But the youngsters needed dances to match the driving music that was burning in their blood, and they got those dances from the same source which originated the jazz that became swing— the black community.

People with very long memories say it began with a dance called the Texas Tommy in the *Darktown Follies* of 1913.

The Texas Tommy's basic step was a kick and a hop three times on each foot, followed by the "breakaway," in which couples separated and each dancer maneuvered individually. Some of the Texas Tommy survived in the Hop which retained the breakaway and added a syncopated two-step or box step accenting the offbeat.

The record business slumped badly in 1932 but soon recovered, and in Lemcke's record store in Webster Groves, Missouri, as elsewhere in the U.S., kids were once again gathering weekly to hear and discuss new releases, perhaps to buy some of them. They bought shrewdly, with an eye to future trades.

Jacob Schneider, a New York attorney and record collector, looks over some of the 450,000 records he stores in the unused ballroom of the old Endicott Hotel. He claims his is the world's largest such collection. To hear them all, a music lover would have to listen steadily 12 hours a day for ten years and three months.

From the Charleston of the '20s, the Hop borrowed the Charleston Swing, a forward and back kick. After Charles Lindbergh's famous solo flight, the Hop became the Lindy Hop. By 1936 it was known as the Jitterbug.

In a slightly modified form, jitterbugging spread to the white world where it was joined by a dance known as the Big Apple which has been traced to a black dance hall in Columbia, South Carolina. Soon the smaller taverns and dance halls were posting apologetic signs: "Sorry, no Big Apple. Not enough room." The Big Apple started when the band leader (or any dancer) cried, "Cut the apple!" and dancers formed circles of eight to ten people each. At the caller's cry of "Come on and swing," the dancers would break into the Charleston Swing, a more violent version of the previous decade's Charleston. Each dancer would step forward on his left foot and kick the right foot up, then step back on the right foot and kick the left foot to the rear. Soon the whole circle would be a flurry of flying feet and counterflying arms and elbows.

When the caller yelled, "Truck to the right!" each dancer would face right, raise an admonitory index finger, step forward and pivot, first on one heel and then on the other. "Truck to the left!" the caller would shout, and the circle would reverse. On "Peck to the east," the dancers would turn their heads to the left and make the chicken-pecking motions celebrated in the highly successful Harry James composition, *Peckin'*. On "Peck to the west!" they would peck right, "And you peck and you peck and you peck your best." At the cry of "Suzy-Q!" each dancer would clasp his hands together and swing his arms to the right while his feet pivoted sideways to the left, like a hammer thrower winding up.

When "Praise Allah!" was the call, the dancers, arms aloft and quivering, rushed together into the center of the circle, chanting "Praise Allah!" In Kickin' the Mule, the boys leapfrogged, and then were leapfrogged by the girls. In the Organ Grinder, each boy knelt on one knee while his partner, with one finger atop his head, trucked around him. Back to the Circle Swing was a hazardous, kicking Charleston with the dancers all facing outward, feet flying wildly. A caller might single out a dancer by name and order him to "shine"—to shag, truck, Suzy-Q or improvise in the center of the ring to the accompaniment of applause and encouraging shouts.

It got into the blood. One coed's father watched his daughter, coming home on vacation from the University of Michigan, truck up to the front door of their house,

TEXT CONTINUED ON PAGE 16

Everyman's Guide to the Lindy

The Lindy Hop, with swing-outs and breakaways added to a basic offbeat two-step, was a permissive dance. Dozens of "shine" steps, including truckin', the shag, the Charleston and the jockey, could be done in any order—not necessarily in the sequence shown here.

③ BREAK GIRL MUST ANTICIPATE (LOOK OUT FOR WHAT BOY WILL DO NEXT)

② STEPPING OUT... INTO...

NOTE SHOULDER

"RUBBING OUT" MOTION ACCENTUATED

TAP TAP

CIGARETTE: NOTE "RUBBING OUT" MOTION

① "READY" POSITION

DANCERS COORDINATE RHYTHM WITH SHOULDER TWITCH AND FOOT TAPS AND THE LIKE. PROCEED TO "RUBBING OUT CIGARETTE" MOTION WHICH IS CONTINUED THROUGHOUT DANCE

NOTE FINGER

ECSTATIC EXPRESSION IS ACCEPTABLE—EVEN DESIRABLE—HERE AND IN #9

NOTE HAND

NOTE LEG

⑦ SWING-OUT (COMPLETION)

⑧ TRUCKIN' (BACK TO BACK OPTIONAL)

FEET ARE SLOSHED AROUND ALTERNATELY AS SHOWN IN DRAWING

*ONLY BOY'S FOOT POSITIONS SHOWN ON DRAWING, AS GIRLS ARE ALL NATURAL-BORN DANCERS

NOTE: #8 AND #9 CAN BE REPLACED BY IMPROVISATIONS IF GIRL AND BOY HAVE HIT IT OFF WELL ON PREVIOUS BREAKS...

NOTE SLOSHING MOTION

13

The Big Apple Blueprinted

The Big Apple, which matured in 1937, allowed for improvisation, as did its predecessor, the Lindy Hop. A group formed a circle, usually facing center, and followed the caller's instructions—tapping the right foot in time to the music or doing the Charleston swing. Later in the dance, the caller might order a Charleston swing facing out, as shown below, a maneuver creating a particular hazard for other dancers.

1.
READY...

GENERAL VIEW OF GROUP PERFORMING ONE OF THE MANY STEPS IN THE BIG APPLE — THE CHARLESTON SWING (SEE INSTRUCTIONAL SEQUENCES). WHEREAS THE TONE OF THE LINDY HOP IS FRANTIC-COOL, SKILL-ORIENTED, THE PRIMARY THRUST OF THE BIG APPLE IS OVERTLY ENERGY-EXPENDING, NEOBUCOLIC, BOISTEROUS

CHARLESTON SWING

1. NEUTRAL POSITION
2. LEFT FOOT FORWARD
3. WEIGHT ON LEFT
4. WEIGHT STILL ON LEFT
5. WEIGHT STILL ON LEFT
6. KICK BACK WITH LEFT / WEIGHT ON RIGHT!

KICKIN' THE MULE

 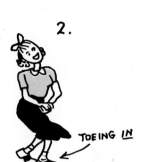  

SUZY-Q

TRUCKIN' (NOTE DROPPED FINAL G)

PECKIN' CHICKEN-LIKE MOTIONS OF HEAD AND NECK

PRAISE ALLAH

A GOOD FINALE: ALL SURGE TOWARD CENTER, HANDS TWITCHING OVERHEAD — THEN BOW LOW, YELLING "PRAISE ALLAH", RAISE ARMS AND BACK OFF

Mimi Elkind of the Bronx (long since become Mimi Lewin) still glows at the memory of 1939 when she danced in the aisles of New York's Paramount Theater to the music of Benny Goodman's band. "I had cut school," she remembers. "Haven't the vaguest idea who the boy was. He was just sitting next to me, and when Gene Krupa's drums rolled out in *Sing, Sing, Sing* we just jumped up and jitterbugged." Mimi's father saw this picture in the New York *Daily News* and bawled her out for skipping school, but after the theater put in its lobby a life-size blowup of Mimi and her partner, her father proudly showed his friends her picture.

then truck through the hallways and upstairs to her bedroom. He turned to his wife and asked, "Is *that* what we're sending her to college for?"

"The names float out of the mist like lost notes," says Lansing Lamont, now a Time-Life News Service correspondent in London, recalling how he used to dance to swing bands as a Boston teen-ager. "Vaughn Monroe playing at the Meadows, somewhere down the Worcester Turnpike about 15 miles from the Hub; Les Brown packing them in at the Totem Pole, a favorite place for high school double-dating. 'The Pole' seemed like the size of Willow Run and on many a Saturday night was one swaying mass of couples mesmerized by Brown's magic. It was not so much the aesthetic experience of listening to Brown's perfect orchestrations as what the mood of his band could do for you and your date. A schmaltzy rendition of *Stardust* could make all the difference between succeeding as a Don Juan or ending the evening with a warm handshake."

The dancing spread uncontrollably, even into the theaters where the big bands played. When Benny Goodman or Harry James was at the Paramount in New York, the kids would start swarming out of the Times Square subways at 4 a.m., their eyes aglow in the morning gloom, ready for the 10 a.m. first show. Zoot-suited boys—green pork-pie hats, yellow coats, pants that seemed to shrink in at the ankles and watch chains that looped down to their knees—lined up at the box office with bobby sox girls. At ten o'clock, the first 4,000 of them squeezed into the theater. Those doomed to wait for succeeding shows pushed and shoved. Once a policeman, pinned against a door jamb, got two ribs fractured.

Inside, the first-show audience patiently endured the movie. Then ushers moved to the edge of the orchestra pit and turned to face the audience, on guard. The curtain rose and there stood the hero of the day—Harry James, say—trumpet to his lips. As the first notes rose higher and higher, the kids swayed to the music, moaned, pulsed and throbbed. They clenched their hands and seethed in their seats. Unable or unwilling to sit still, they jitterbugged in the aisles, shagged in the balconies and boxes and stayed for show after show.

"It was all there," recalls Lans Lamont. "Within eight blocks were the Capitol, Roxy, Loew's, Paramount and Strand theaters. You had your pick of the big bands: James, Goodman, the Dorsey brothers, Lionel Hampton, Charlie Barnet and Gene Krupa. If you were lucky enough to get in, you lived in the theater for days on end. Nothing today can recapture that pause when the film had ended, the last chords of the organ had reverberated through the theater and then it came: Goodman's clarinet lilting *Let's Dance* or Charlie Barnet's saxophone shouting out *Cherokee*. You sat bolt upright, nudging your schoolmate and unconsciously beginning to pound your feet in rhythm. The stage lights burst aglow and out of the pit rose this marvelous ark filled with 16 or 20 men, their gleaming golden instruments flashing in the spotlights that bathed the whole scene.

"There was hardly time to catch your breath—the band was already pulsating with life, the front sax section filling the hall with sweet notes, the brass setting your ears afire, Buddy Rich or Jo Jones flailing their snares, tom-toms and cymbals, a row of trombonists executing precision drill, Charlie Shavers or Cootie Williams piercing the rafters with a pure paroxysm of trumpet joy."

Everywhere from theater aisles to living-room floors sprinkled with sugar to reduce friction, white youngsters were doing the black-inspired dances of the day, while black youngsters were adding even greater inspiration to the original conceptions. One of the best places to see this phenomenon in action was Harlem's marvelous Savoy Ballroom, which ran from 140th to 141st Street on Lenox Avenue. A great marble stairway led to a vast room with space for tables and chairs and 10,000 square feet for dancing. Colored spotlights played intermittently on the dancers. A well-stocked ice-cream soda fountain offered chocolate-nut sundaes, banana splits and floats. Mostly what it sold was ginger-ale setups into which the customers poured their own portable potables while listening to Ella Fitzgerald's effortless singing and Chick Webb driving hard ahead on his snare and bass drums and flicking his sticks over the cymbals. The night Chick's band "battled" Benny Goodman's, 4,000 people crowded into the Savoy and even more (some say 25,000) gathered outside.

Many whites came to the Savoy to fox-trot or to listen to Ella and Chick. More came just to watch young black couples whirling through stylized, intricate and very, very fast dances. Shorty Snowden, king of the Savoy dancers, once said, "I used to dance seven complete choruses of *Bugle Blues* or *Tiger Rag* in a minute and three quarters, which was considered sensational." It *was* sensational.

"I've put together new steps in the breakaway by slipping and almost falling," Shorty continued. "I was al-

The swinging zoot suit had an in-and-out history. It emerged in 1942 only to be banned by the War Production Board as flagrantly un-austere. After the war it re-emerged briefly, then was folded away again.

ways looking for anyone dancing in the street, or just walking or doing anything that suggests a step. If I could see it, I could do it." After Snowden met Paul Draper, the great white dancer, some of Draper got into Shorty's version of the Hop. "Especially," Shorty said, "a running floor slide combined with a knee lock."

The kind of dancing Shorty and others perfected was "choreographed swing music," wrote the late Marshall Stearns and Jean Stearns in *Jazz Dance*. Younger dancers like Al Minns, Joe Daniels, Russel Williams and Pepsi Bethel produced the Back Flip, the Over the Head and the Snatch. Girls flew through the air as if shot from cannons. Musicians and dancers stimulated each other. "Great dancers make you swing," Duke Ellington once said, and Louis Armstrong and Jack Teagarden both have said they preferred to play for dancers.

The Savoy's floor was something special. "That floor was built to vibrate," trombonist Dicky Wells recalls in his book, *The Night People*, "but I didn't know it. I was standing by the bandstand and it started to vibrate, that floor was loaded so. I came out of there and didn't find out about it being a sprung floor until a year later. Yeah, I vibrated on out the door!" At the Savoy the real jitterbugs danced five nights a week to music provided by two alternating bands. The music never stopped. At the end of an evening even the dancers' shoes would be sopping wet.

The dancers rested on Wednesday and Friday nights, which were reserved for private social affairs at the Savoy. Mondays, Tuesdays and Thursdays they came early because the admission price rose at 6 p.m. from 30 cents to 60 cents and rose again at 8 to 85 cents. Monday was Ladies Night and Thursday was Kitchen Mechanics Night, when maids and cooks had the night off. The crowds were thin then, and the relatively open dance floor was great for practice.

On Saturdays the middle-aged white squares showed up to watch the dancers. On Saturday afternoons the dancers sent their best clothes out to be pressed for Sunday night. In their second-best suits they gathered in front of the Savoy, wisecracking and waiting for manager Charles Buchanan to rush out and offer to pay them to go in and dance for the people.

On Sundays, dancers, musicians and actors from Broadway shows jammed the Savoy. Now, dressed in their best, dancers executed steps too fast for the eye to follow. Shorty Snowden tightly clutched his partner, Big Bea, who was a foot taller than he, while his feet shot out in all directions. Stretch Jones danced with Little Bea, who was a foot shorter than he and was always getting lost. The folks from downtown loved it and showered tips upon the dancers. The northeast corner of the ballroom was the Cats' Corner, where only the best dancers could sit or dance. A poor dancer blundering into this sacred region was ignored. A good dancer moving in was considered an invader and was

promptly discouraged, often by gracefully administered Charleston kicks to the shins. Any dancer who copied another dancer's specialty risked being tromped on by the crowd.

Most of the men who set the land to dancing and listening to swing started as boys consumed with a desire to make music.

Arranger Larry Wagner, who wrote *No Name Jive* for Glen Gray's Casa Loma Orchestra, says, "I learned trumpet by myself from a book. I'd practice all day. You've got to be greedy to practice to be an instrumen-

Most ballroom Lindy Hoppers stayed on the ground. Some experts took to the air. In the "round-the-back" demonstrated here by Harlem dancers Leon James and Willa Mae Ricker, the dancers start with the swing-out. Then Willa Mae moves closer for a take-off and Leon swings her over his back, guiding her flight with his arms, back to the floor for the next fancy figure.

Leon and Willa Mae cut many a fantastic step. Leon executes *(top left)* a spectacular high kick. In a variation on the Charleston *(left center)*, he sends Willa Mae soaring high astride his limber right leg. Then, as Willa Mae steadies him and helps pull him along,

he throws himself into a heel-and-toe slide *(bottom left)*. If the floor was slick enough, his slide could carry him the length of a block-long ballroom. In a felicitous finale *(above)*, Leon and Willa Mae jump high into the air in an exuberant gesture of pure dancing joy.

talist." Sidney Bechet at six would sneak his older brother's clarinet out of a dresser drawer and practice under the porch. Louis Armstrong remembered: "I had an awful urge to learn the cornet."

Tens of thousands of kids hopefully joined forces in thousands of local dance units. Most of them, of course, were destined to go nowhere and their earnings were miniscule. At least one outfit contrived to *lose* money. This went under the name of Bill Gold and His Pieces of Eight—perhaps in itself a reason sufficient to put it into the red. The location was McKeesport, a steel, tin and coal town not far from Pittsburgh, Pennsylvania. The time was the Depression. The Pieces of Eight put up hard-cadged money to buy stock arrangements, practiced diligently on the instruments purchased by culture-oriented parents, hoping they had spawned Heifetzes or Damrosches. More: they hired halls, themselves waxed the floors, paid for posters and tickets. Every weekend. And no one ever came. No one. Pianist Bill dropped his ambitions for a career in music, and even dropped his first name in the career he did adopt.

Out in Missoula, Montana, Alan Merriam played clarinet in various high school and college bands, doing Saturday-night gigs in Indian reservation towns and helping the bass player get his instrument out through the back window when fights started. The crowds didn't always like the swing the kids were trying to play. Sometimes the band had to cozen a backwoods audience by announcing, "And in our next number we will feature Harold Herbig who will play his solo with his *eyes shut!*" This always stunned the locals. The band rented a bus and spent all of one summer gigging around Montana. At the end of the season they divided the profit. It came to $2 each. "It was better than not playing," says Merriam.

Many swing musicians worked their way up through the studio bands in radio stations. These jobs paid well and the hours were reasonable, but they bored most sidemen stiff. They usually had to play pretty dull music (though they managed to slip in many a good riff) and their musical judgment was often overridden by sponsors and advertising executives. Most of the best musicians were attracted to the big swing bands whose life was glamorous though often tough, and the music was challenging but fun. For many, the big band bus was a way out of a dull little hometown.

A young musician found that in a band he was one of a large family of talented people, sharing all the problems engendered by artistic sensitivity and close proximity. There was much warm affection. To be with friends, men quit good jobs or stuck with foundering bands. But there were also rivalries, childish jealousies, cliques, intrigues and a great and often resented dependence upon that father figure, the bandleader.

"There were always these politicians that spoiled the band," says William S. ("Popsie") Randolph, Benny

Lucky Millinder's band traveled in the battered bus shown above. "You could not stand up in it," drummer Panama Francis says. It was triple-decked with bunks for nights when the band could find no hotel rooms.

Goodman's longtime band boy. "A guy will say to another guy, 'You ought to be getting more money. I can't live on the road on what I get. How do you manage?' And the other guy will say, 'Yeah, I oughta be getting more.' And then the trouble starts."

Says Yank Lawson: "The night we joined the Tommy Dorsey band Tommy offered to take us to hear his brother Jimmy, and Buddy Morrow said, 'No, thanks, I don't go out with leaders.' I don't think Tommy ever forgot that."

"Musicians are a strange and jealous lot," the Casa Loma Band's Glen Gray once said. "If the saxophonist gets more opportunities to show off than does the trumpeter, that's the beginning of a feud."

Two sidemen might get along musically but not otherwise, or vice versa. A New Yorker Hotel audience was once astonished to see a clarinetist and a trumpeter fly at each other's throats, accusing each other of having loused up the set. Sidemen were adept at sabotage. Buddy Rich kept playing little drum riffs during tender

moments in Frank Sinatra's ballads, even after Frank reportedly punched his nose. But years later Frankie helped finance Buddy's new band.

A few musicians, mostly bandleaders, developed hobbies outside music. Harry James played baseball fanatically. Guy Lombardo raced speedboats and Frank Trumbauer and Orville Knapp flew airplanes for sport. Jack Teagarden tinkered with cars and Tex Beneke with ham radios. But most musicians found it hard to develop interests outside the band. In the opening weeks of 1940, Glenn Miller's men played two daily sessions totaling five hours of music (six on weekends) in the Cafe Rouge of the Hotel Pennsylvania in New York. They also played three radio programs weekly, each preceded by a long rehearsal, plus four, and sometimes five, shows daily at the Paramount Theater, and in their spare time recorded nearly 30 sides of 78-rpm records.

Even more demanding was the road, say a Christmas-season tour in unreliable cars through snowy, icy Pennsylvania with Glenn Miller, or 30 consecutive one-night

Bands often hit rough roads. When Millinder's bus broke down, the sidemen thumbed rides from farm trucks, as in the picture above, to their next night's gig.

these guys trying to climb on while the stage was going up and them knocking over music stands and all. Sometimes they wouldn't show up at all and I'd have to get on the stand and hold an instrument, not play, just hold it to fill up a chair."

If a band got into town early the musicians would sit in the hotel lobby until the cheaper day rates began, since sidemen usually paid their own expenses on the road and the price of a hotel room could be important. Many a sideman was broke before he got his pay, which came weekly with most bands but nightly with some struggling bands which might not have another engagement that week or whose members had less than complete faith in the financial probity of the leader.

Usually a band arrived for an engagement in mid-afternoon, too late to go to a hotel. At the job site the musicians would set up their instruments and music, test the permanent public address system and, if it was inadequate, install their own portable system. Then they would rush to find tailors to press tuxedoes and to freshen up the girl singer's filmy gown. Often none was available, and the sidemen, having eaten quickly in the handiest greasy spoon, would rush to the ballroom and struggle in rest rooms to revive their clothes. By eight o'clock they were on the bandstand, as trim and fresh-looking as possible.

Keeping natty could be an economic problem. When the Casa Loma Orchestra first appeared in white ties and tails, some of the men had to adopt weird crouching postures on the stand. They had tails but no socks. When Eddie Condon was playing with Artie Shaw's band at New York's Paramount Theater, the sidemen were wearing brown suede shoes. Eddie and drummer George Wettling hit on a thrifty scheme. Eddie's feet were hidden during the performance except for one moment when he put his right foot on a chair and played a 16-bar solo. Wettling's right foot was hidden throughout; his left was exposed. For that engagement they shared one pair of brown suede shoes.

The starchiest band on the road

One critic always remembered a particular band as being sloppy because the first time he saw them they looked haggard and unpressed. He never knew that the band had eaten little for nine days and had not a dime to spare for pressing. Even when a band had time and money for laundering, things sometimes went wrong. One band manager, during a long stretch on the road, left all the band's laundry outside his hotel-room door in one immense bundle marked "No starch." Two sidemen returning late and in very high good humor changed the instructions to "Heavy starch." The band wore sheet-iron-stiff shirts for the rest of the trip.

The road manager was vital to band logistics. Before a long train trip Popsie would find out if the railroad planned, along the way, to switch off the baggage car

stands through the broiling summertime Midwest with Benny Goodman. When the next engagement was no more than 200 miles away, the sidemen, after a late supper and perhaps a jam session with men from any other nearby band, would sleep a few hours in a hotel and leave next day by bus or in their own cars. But often the overnight jump was 300 or 400 miles, and the band, after finishing its engagement at 2 a.m., would dine, either jam or rehearse, and by 4 a.m. at least some of the band would be ready to drive through the night. As trumpeter Shorty Sherock, a veteran of half a dozen top bands, remembers it: "Everybody was there except the girl singer. She was always late." Girl singers say they were always prompt.

Somebody had to ride herd on the sidemen most of the time. Popsie recalls how it was when he was acting as road manager for Goodman: "If the bus left at 3 p.m. I'd tell them to be there at 10:30 a.m., because if you say 3 then some of them won't show until 7 p.m. Sometimes they'd surprise you and all show up at 10:30 a.m. Then I'd just start the trip early.

"When we were playing the Paramount the first show would start at 10:45-11 a.m. I'd call some of these guys at the hotel and say, 'The show's starting'; and they'd say, 'OK,' and go back to sleep. And then the stage would start to go up and here would come some of containing the instruments and attach it to some later train bound for the same destination. If so, Popsie would give up his roomette and sleep in the baggage car. "I'd wake up and smell flowers and look around and the rest of the car would be full of coffins and flowers." But when the car was switched Popsie would be there, handing out bribes and getting the instruments onto the next available train so that they always arrived on time. "Some of those other bands, they'd get there and have to borrow instruments from some high school band and fake it," he recalls. "But not us."

Haircuts and crap games on the bus

Musicians spent their bus time sleeping, playing cards, reading, eating and drinking. Some sneaked an occasional joint of marijuana, then called "tea," among other names. Sometimes they cut each other's hair. They gambled constantly. Shorty Sherock remembers the day a musician brought some toy racing cars aboard the bus. The sidemen lined up the cars at the rear of the center aisle and placed their bets. On signal the bus driver slammed on his brakes and the little cars went flying down the aisle. At the end of that lively trip the bus's brakes were completely shot.

Dice and cards were the more usual implements of chance. Billie Holiday related in her book, *Lady Sings the Blues,* a memorable crap game in Count Basie's bus: "I was on my knees in the bottom of that bus from West Virginia to New York, a few hundred miles and about twelve hours. When we pulled up in front of the Woodside Hotel everybody was broke and crying. I was filthy dirty and had holes in the knees of my stockings, but I had sixteen hundred bucks and some change."

A bus trip could be a nightmare. Benny Goodman in *The Kingdom of Swing* recalled the rickety bus he once hired to take his first band to a one-nighter in Johnson City, New York, on Christmas night: "We hadn't traveled outside the city when we discovered there was no heat in the bus. Then it started to snow, and here we were crawling along about 15 or 18 miles an hour. Johnson City is up around Binghamton, with hills all the way. Going up, we had to get out and walk on some of them. Coming down, the brakes didn't hold and we skidded all over the road, bumping a truck once and breaking some of the back windows. To top things off, the driver had never been outside of New York, and he would make a wrong turn every so often. . . .

"We were due at the place to start playing at eight, but what with one thing and another, it was 11:45 before we got there, with everybody squawking about the bus, half-frozen, and in just the mood to play. . . . The next day we came home on the train."

Yank Lawson remembers a cold trip with Tommy Dorsey's band: "I went to sleep with my face against the bus window and got Bell's palsy. The nerves were frozen. I had a solo and I came out without warming up

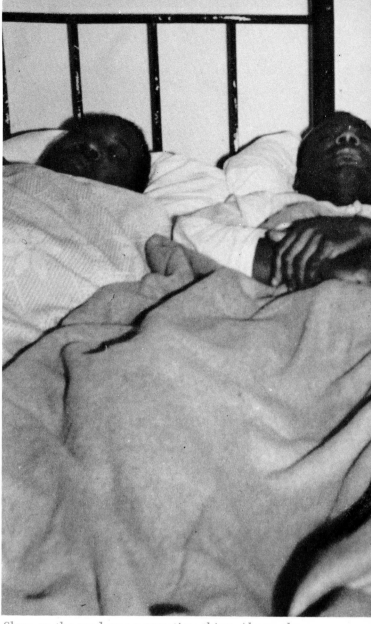

Sleep on the road was a sometime thing. Above, three sidemen of the Lucky Millinder band share two beds in

or anything and started to blow and it just went 'foooot.' Nothing came out. Tommy said, 'Why don't you get some sleep?' I couldn't play for eight weeks and Tommy paid all the bills."

Gene Krupa, now firmly settled in Yonkers, New York, says: "That life was so full of greasy spoons and bad food. You yearned for a night off and when you got it you'd get so drunk you wouldn't know what was going on anyway. I used to look at the lighted windows of the homes and yearn for the same kind of life."

Arranger-composer Eddie Sauter was blowing trumpet with the Charlie Barnet band in 1935 when, as he recalls, the band was fired by the Hotel Roosevelt in New Orleans after one night. (Barnet says the band played there six weeks; perhaps it just *seemed* like six weeks because the band was unpopular.) Sauter joined Barnet's next band, which was fired after a week in Bar Harbor, Maine, because it couldn't play enough like

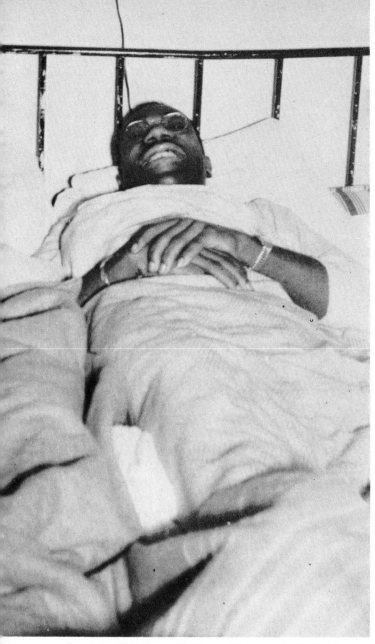

the Star Hotel in El Paso, Texas, which broke its whites-only rule for Millinder. Drowsing at right are

three Bob Crosby sidemen: drummer Ray Bauduc, clarinetist Irving Fazola and trombonist Warren Smith.

Rudy Vallee's. "It was the strawberry season, and we were so broke that I remember living on flounder and strawberries," Sauter recalls.

Shorty Sherock's longest road trip was with Krupa's band in Pennsylvania and West Virginia: two and a half weeks of one-nighters without checking into a hotel. "We slept in the bus, washed up and shaved in men's rooms. When we got to Washington there were no hotel rooms because the war was on and military people had priority. So we drove out to the Washington Monument. Everybody picked out a comfortable tree and went to sleep underneath it with the bus seats as pillows. We finally played the job and got top performances from everybody."

Some bands practically never left the road. In an average year, Jimmie Lunceford's band covered 40,000 miles to play 200 one-night stands, 15 weeks of theater and a four-week ballroom gig. When World War II

swept many swing musicians into the armed forces, some of them found dodging buzz bombs in England with Glenn Miller's band or island-hopping with Bob Crosby's only slightly more arduous than peacetime working conditions.

Along with the other difficulties and dangers of the musical life, the color bar was, for black musicians, a constant irritation, a frequent humiliation and an occasional deadly hazard. Black bands could not get jobs at the best white hotels or get meals or beds at most white restaurants or hotels. A black band arriving in a new town usually checked in with the leading black citizen, the preacher or the undertaker, who knew which homes would take black paying guests. Duke Ellington's great band played Loew's State Theater on Broadway in 1938 but not the Paramount or the Strand, the big show houses then specializing in swing bands.

Recording executive John Hammond recalls his

struggles to find New York restaurants which would take black diners. He helped to launch one such place—Cafe Society Downtown which was followed by Cafe Society Uptown—but even there the management had trouble keeping waiters from steering all black customers to balcony tables.

Hammond was a leader in erasing the color bar. The musicians themselves had begun the process in the early days of jazz when white musicians began listening to and learning from the jazz masters of New Orleans. In the Swing Era, blacks and whites mingled in after-hours jam sessions to play for their own pleasure. There were even Friday-morning jam sessions on the stage of Harlem's Apollo Theater until the musicians' union ruled that playing to paying customers for free was musical madness.

A few bold recording companies cut records, and some radio stations did broadcasts with mixed bands without identifying the invisible performers—but nobody would hire a mixed band for public performance. Hammond created a scandal in Mount Kisco, New York, high society when he hired for a country-club dance a band which included such great black jazzmen as Fats Waller, drummer Zutty Singleton, alto saxist Benny Carter and trumpeter Frankie Newton, as well as whites like guitarist Eddie Condon, bassist Artie Bernstein and clarinetist Pee Wee Russell. "I remember getting two quarts of Gordon's gin for Fats," says Hammond, "poured into a water pitcher, so it looked like water, and by the time he got to the piano he was all over it. The kids loved the music; the adults hated it. Since my father was president of the club, they couldn't do anything to me."

Eddie Condon's mixed-band Town Hall concerts helped, too, and so did Duke Ellington's triumphal tours of Europe. Duke was received as an honored guest in royal palaces and in the homes of the rich and famous. The tours helped him to get bookings in some of the better U.S. hotels.

At Hammond's urging, Benny Goodman hired some great black arrangers like Fletcher Henderson and Edgar Sampson. Other bands followed his lead and Chick Webb completed the circle by hiring a white arranger, Van Alexander. Goodman pioneered again by hiring Teddy Wilson and Lionel Hampton, and again other bands followed his lead. But life was still a little extra tough for black musicians. On one of the Good-

In World War II more than 4,500 musicians and entertainers worked in battle areas and found that travel conditions were not too different from what bands had experienced at home in peacetime. Here the cast of a USO musical comedy is sacked out on the floor and atop the baggage in a Navy plane bound for Guam.

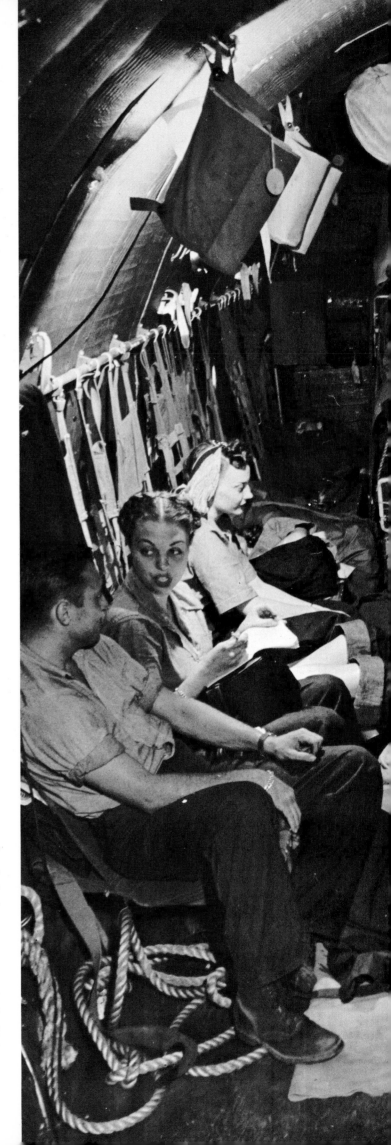

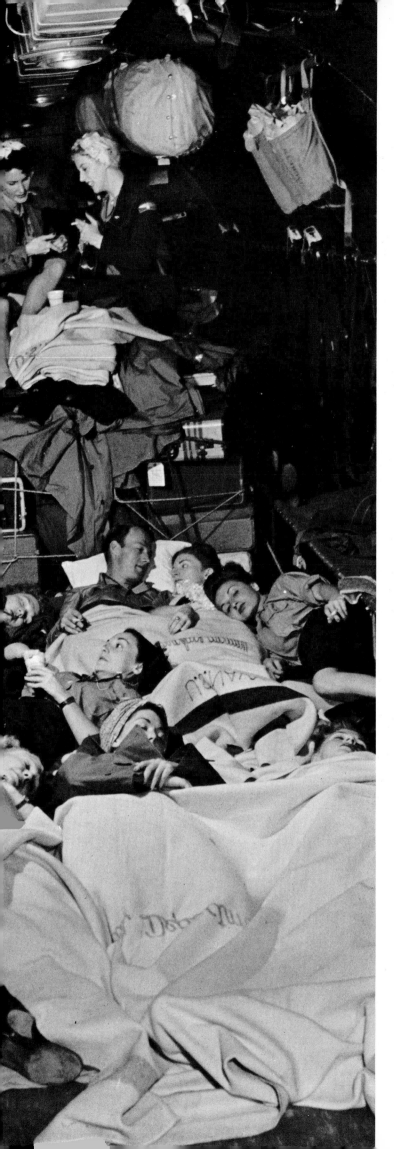

man band's southern gigs Lionel Hampton was rescued from the harassments of two local cops only because the chief of police was a jazz fan.

Dicky Wells recalls that many black musicians returning safely from a tour of the South used to kiss the sidewalks of New York. "In those days, when we were traveling in the South, most cats had firearms somewhere, somehow," he recalls; "The ofays would try to frighten you if somebody got out of line, and want to beat up the band or shoot somebody."

Billie Holiday remembered a Southern tour with Artie Shaw's band: "It got to the point where I hardly ever ate, slept or went to the bathroom without having a major NAACP-type production." The North was often no better. A Detroit theater manager made Billie wear dark make-up because she looked too light-skinned to him to be singing with Count Basie's black band. When she sang with Shaw in a New York hotel, the manager made her enter and leave by the back door. Lena Horne recalls her fury at being asked to sing to black GIs and finding that the camp commander had filled the front seats with German prisoners of war; blacks sat in the rear. Lena got down off the stage, went out into the audience, turned her back on the Germans and sang to her countrymen.

Pearl Bailey remembers being refused service by a waiter in a Chinese restaurant in Chicago. "He started with the language I couldn't understand, but he kept ending with, 'Me no serve.' That did it. I told him in a slow Oriental drawl, 'You think I came to America to pick cotton. I was told you came to do laundry, so, brother, serve.' And you know what? He did."

For all their hard work, few sidemen got rich playing with the big bands even in their palmiest days and fewer still were astute money managers. The American Federation of Musicians, through its local unions, helped musicians to get at least a living wage, though "union scale" varied widely, not only from city to city but between black and white locals and between different places of entertainment in the same town. AFM President James Caesar Petrillo achieved better returns for musicians from radio and recording work, though his ban on instrumental recordings, affecting most of the record companies for 27 long months, was one of the blows, like wartime rationing and changes in public taste, that combined to kill the big bands.

Odd hours and long trips made normal family life impossible for musicians. Many married sidemen fretted over the possible infidelities of their wives, perhaps because they were not above a bit of romance on the road themselves. One famous brass man had a pair of alligator shoes, too good for road trips, which he left at home with his wife. He returned from one trip to find that a fellow musician had been making free not only with his wife but with his alligator shoes. The friend was contrite. "I couldn't help it," he said, of the brief affair, "it was *so* good." Said the brass man later, "Well, I couldn't shank him for that. But I sure gave him hell about those alligator shoes."

The life drove many to drink, some of them heavily. An often-repeated story has it that the late Bunny Berigan, well into the sauce, once leaned back a little too far before launching into a trumpet solo in New York's Paramount Theater and fell six feet from his perch on the band platform onto the stage. But few sidemen thought of abandoning the swinging life. "What do you suppose Guy Lombardo's drummer tells people he does for a living?" they used to ask each other. Not all were great artists. "For every top man in the bands I've worked," says bandleader Thad Jones, "there were three or four you wondered where they came from." But there were an astonishing number of good ones. Some are retired, many work daytimes at more prosaic jobs but still go out on gigs nights and weekends and many are working fulltime in radio, TV, recording and film studios, at the clubs in Las Vegas, Lake Tahoe and Reno or in the big bands of such still-active leaders as Duke Ellington, Harry James and Count Basie.

The sidemen who make the re-creations for this series are nearly all veterans of swing, all full-time working musicians, squeezing in these recording sessions in the evenings. Some, like Skeets Herfurt, come to Los Angeles from as far away as Lake Tahoe to re-create the music they lived in the '30s and '40s.

In addition to sidemen, a swing band needed singers. Sidemen who also sang usually got along well with their peers but most musicians looked down on "boy" and "girl" singers who did nothing but sing. A girl singer had the special problem of being a lone woman in a busload of men. She could build a wall of ice around herself or become one of the boys, but either way was likely to be criticized by the sidemen. A third desperate option was to fall in love with one of the musicians.

Some singers had tough starts. Frank Sinatra, training for the future, sang 18 radio shows weekly at such hours as dawn, noon and 5 p.m. for free, just to get the exposure. Ella Fitzgerald, in her first amateur-night appearance at the Harlem Opera House, was too scared to do the dance number she had planned. She sang instead, got a chance to appear with Chick Webb's band at Yale, knocked the undergraduates dead and was on her way.

Bandleaders had their favorite singers and singers had their favorite bandleaders. Helen Forrest was in such demand that she became the only girl to have sung with the Artie Shaw, Harry James and Benny Goodman bands. Many of his former sidemen are critical of Benny Goodman, but girls like Helen Ward and Louise Tobin remember him as a wonderful boss. Peggy Lee thinks the BG band was the best support a girl ever had. "The big band era gave a singer a grounding you couldn't beat," she says. "Just to sit there on the bandstand and listen to that music and those musicians!"

Glenn Miller signs autographs for his admirers at the Meadowbrook ballroom. A bandleader had to meet and greet the public as well as produce memorable music.

Sometimes the routine got to a singer. Kenny Sargent played sax and sang in the Casa Loma Orchestra. He must have sung *For You* thousands of times, but one night he got up, sang 16 bars of it—and sat down. "I forgot the words," he said. The words were often very forgettable. "Lyrics were always a means to an end for me," said Helen Ward. "Some of them were lovely, they made sense. But many were just plain stupid. Take the song *Martha,* which was strictly a man's song. I was annoyed that I had to sing the tune at all, so I used to

sing 'Arthur, Arthur.'" But Bob Eberly thinks lyrics added to the romantic mood of the music.

Singers bravely sang cryptic lyrics like "Mairzy Doats and Dozy Doats" and baby-talk lyrics like the ones about the "fee itty fitty" in the "itty bitty poo" and strictly nonsense lyrics like "The Flat Foot Floogee with the Floy Floy" and "Hut-Sut Rawl-son on the rill-er-ah."

What made a good bandleader? Perfectionists like Goodman, Miller and Tommy Dorsey produced thrilling music in a tense atmosphere. Under more relaxed

Among the best vocalists of the Swing Era were Lena Horne *(left, below)* shown singing Cole Porter's *Let's Do It;* Bonnie Baker *(center, below)* whose baby-voiced version of *Oh Johnny* with Orrin Tucker's band sold half a million records; and Billie Holiday *(right, below),* seen with Ben Webster *(left)* and others of Willie Bryant's band. With Glenn Miller's band *(bottom left)* at the Meadowbrook are singers Marion Hutton and Ray Eberle. Composer-vocalist Johnny Mercer sings along *(bottom right)* with pianist Willie ("The Lion") Smith.

leaders like Henderson, Count Basie, Jimmy Dorsey and Ellington, bands also made thrilling music and seemed to be having more fun.

A leader had to help to project to the public an image of a band with a unique and thrilling sound. He also had to persuade somebody to finance the band's beginning, deal daily with the personal problems of the sidemen, confer with the band's manager, the band boy, the booking agents and the managers of places where bands played. He had to work with record-company and radio-station executives, and in his spare moments he was expected with charming ease to sign autographs.

Duke Ellington has proved that a fine musician who can write with exquisite sensibility for the various skills of his sidemen can also be a great bandleader. But Cab Calloway, who could not arrange anything or play an instrument, except for occasional attempts on the drums, once told an interviewer: "A band must consist of good musicians, must have top-flight arrangements, must be well-rehearsed and competently led. But that isn't enough. . . . People can't be held and entertained in the complete sense by sound alone. There must be something for the eyes to see. . . ."

Calloway was something to see. A tall, handsome man with a million-dollar smile and a happy, friendly air, he would launch the band into action, then, with elbows flying, would furiously dance out from under his hat.

Spiffy music czar Petrillo enters his office. His ban on recordings deprived bands for a time of an important segment of their audience and helped to kill big bands.

The crowds gone and night spots dark, a single cop guards New York's Swing Street in the late '40s. Mayor

William O'Dwyer closed the clubs because of wartime fuel shortages; none survive today on 52nd Street.

Once he danced off the bandstand and broke an ankle. He would encourage soloists with great roaring shouts. And he would get a stranglehold on a microphone and sing. Once he forgot the words and sang "Hi-de-ho," the phrase which eventually became his trademark.

Bands depended heavily on arrangers, composers and lyricists. Arrangers were usually capable sidemen who could read and write music easily, knew what each instrument could and could not do, and were sensitive to the musical strengths and weaknesses of the band members. Arranging could be frustrating. Eddie Sauter, who has written music for many bands, who has led his own band with Bill Finegan and who is greatly respected among swing musicians, sees his life in swing as one long battle between his highly original ideas and the demand for more commercial music: "Any arranging I was ever satisfied with was undercover; it got in sidewise."

Some arrangers got on particularly well with bandleaders. Duke Ellington and Billy Strayhorn became musically almost indistinguishable. Sauter, who suffered long bouts of tuberculosis, remembers Goodman gratefully. "Benny kept me a whole year on my income —$75 a week—while I was ill. He also went out of his way to visit me." Most arrangers also liked to compose and some of them added greatly to the stream of fresh, new sound the bands needed to keep swing alive. Duke Ellington's torrent of original numbers has placed him high among American composers, and men like Sy Oliver, Larry Clinton, Gene Gifford, Edgar Sampson, Eddie Sauter and Johnny Mercer also increased the sparkle of the Swing Era.

Johnny Mercer sang with the Paul Whiteman band and in radio shows with Benny Goodman and Bob Crosby. After hours he sang for fun in New York's 52nd Street night spots. He has more than a thousand songs to his credit, 80 percent being his words to other people's music and 20 percent being his words and his music. On songwriting for the big bands, Johnny says: "God, it was hard. I was so young. I started at 15 and had my first song, *Out of Breath and Scared to Death of You*, published at 21. Writing song titles is the hardest part and writing funny lyrics and a good ballad is the toughest. You can be given a tune you are not fond of and have to write the words. But if you know the composer well enough you can tell him it isn't such a good tune and he'll give you a better one. Jerome Kern wouldn't mind, for instance. Words are tougher to do than music.

"I have a good ear, but I can't play the piano. Paul Weston took down *Dream* for me. I sort of hit the chords with my fists. I write notes in a sort of shorthand. Then I either play the piece to a publisher with one finger or bring a pianist along to play it.

"*Lazy Bones* took the longest to write. It took a year and Hoagy Carmichael helped a lot. That song really started me off and I am deeply appreciative. But *Days of Wine and Roses* came pouring out in ten minutes. It was as if someone was dictating to me."

After all the necessary ingredients had been assembled, a band still needed financing and a place to play. Too often, places which hired bands were gangster-controlled, a situation which began with mob-run speakeasies and continued after Prohibition ended, with gangster domination of some of the nightclubs in Manhattan, and in Detroit, Minneapolis, Chicago, Kansas City and Boston.

In Chicago the Cotton Club, Friar's Inn, Grand Terrace and the Pekin Cafe (later replaced for a time by, of all things, a police station) were all hangouts of gangster Al Capone or his brother Ralph ("Bottles") Capone. In the heart of Harlem, gangsters Owney Madden and "Big Frenchy" De Mange hired burly bouncers under Herman Stark to keep all but the affluent blacks out of their Cotton Club.

Lena Horne was still a Cotton Club chorus girl when she scored a hit singing a duet, *As Long as I Live*, with Avon Long. She wanted to try for a singing job elsewhere, so her stepfather, a fierce little Cuban named Miguel Rodriguez, asked the club's bosses for her release—"a little too forcefully," Lena has recalled. "Some of their boys followed him out into the street and beat him up very severely. Next day, one of the bosses came to me and said, 'Who do you think you are? You know you can't work anywhere but here.'" Lena had to run away to get a full-time singing job on the road with Noble Sissle's band.

Gangster interests behind the Cotton Club used a judicious display of mob muscle to wrench Duke Ellington away from a Philadelphia theater which had him under contract. Another gang found a gracious old house with white columns near the Cotton Club and set up the competing Plantation Club. They hired Cab Calloway, a recent Cotton Club star. Cab got to play just two nights. Then rival gangsters wrecked the Plantation Club and murdered Harry Block, one of its principal backers.

The bands behind the bands

Fortunately mob interests did not extend to all branches of the music business, and though bands often complained (sometimes with justice) of rapacious or indifferent management, band financing was largely outside the criminal orbit. Financing for bands came sometimes from another band as it did when Benny Goodman backed Harry James or when Glenn Miller backed Charlie Spivak and Hal McIntyre. Sometimes it came from people with great confidence in their own musical taste and commercial instincts, like Si Shribman who, with his brother Charlie, owned or operated a chain of New England ballrooms. The bands of Tony Pastor, Artie Shaw, Glenn Miller, Woody Herman and Claude Thornhill, all started with Shribman money and

Shribman bookings. Si could book them not only into his own ballrooms but into most New England colleges where they met their natural audience, the kids.

John Hammond, whose name inevitably comes up in any discussion of Benny Goodman, Count Basie or the beginnings of swing in general, deserves extensive discussion as the archetype of activist buff. As a boy, he used to pass Harlem's Alhambra Theater on 125th Street on his way to his viola teacher's Riverside Drive studio. He took to dropping off the streetcar and visiting the Alhambra where he fell in love with jazz. He began to buy "race" records, the music of Negro artists then bought by few whites. He toured Harlem with Artie Bernstein, later Goodman's bassist, and got to know the black musicians.

The scout behind the newspaper

As a young man with a private income, he became a musical scout, driving off in his car or flying to Kansas City, Galveston or the Pacific coast, wherever anyone was blowing a hot horn. He could be an unnerving listener, sitting at a nightclub table and reading a newspaper while a band played, but if he liked the music, the musicians soon got offers of jobs and bookings, introductions to new players and better vocalists. Hammond accepted no commissions for this promotional work, and when he became American recording director for the English division of Columbia Records, he used his musical protégés as often as he could to make jazz records for sale in England. He energetically promoted the Goodman and Basie bands, as well as the careers of Teddy Wilson, Charlie Christian, Lionel Hampton and boogie-woogie pianists Meade Lux Lewis, Albert Ammons and Pete Johnson and has never stopped crusading for good music.

The swing scene was covered journalistically only by a handful of knowledgeable reporters. These writers knew what the music was all about, and though their reviews could dissect a band pitilessly, their magazines' popularity polls and annual awards meant kudos, publicity and, inevitably, money to winning musicians. Sidemen might complain about some of the notices but most of them respected the coverage of *Down Beat* and *Metronome,* the only important magazines which consistently chronicled the swing scene, as well as the occasional pieces in *The New Yorker* and *Esquire.*

Not only musicians read the swing magazines. Fans followed their columns devotedly and some enthusiasts still treasure complete files of these periodicals.

As has already been chronicled elsewhere in this series, World War II saw the beginning of the decline of the Big Bands of the Swing Era. Many sidemen went into the service; the bands that remained had to fight increased taxes, gasoline rationing and, in some areas, the blackout or brownout. To these troubles were added wars within the music industry. The American Society of Composers, Authors and Publishers (ASCAP) asked radio stations and networks to pay more for the privilege of broadcasting music by ASCAP members. The fight kept ASCAP tunes off the air for ten months in 1941 and led to a proliferation of swing versions of traditional numbers like *Jeanie with the Light Brown Hair.* Earlier in the Swing Era, Tommy Dorsey had been cut off the air for swinging *Loch Lomond,* because a radio station manager thought that listeners of Scottish extraction might be offended, but now people were used to it.

Another musical war broke out when James Caesar Petrillo, president of the American Federation of Musicians, called a strike against the recording companies in an effort to win royalties for the musicians, most of whom earned nothing from a record except the recording fee. It was more than two years before all the companies agreed to his demands and during that time the vocalists, who did not belong to the AFM, had largely supplanted bands in the recording studios. Public taste, too, had turned away from swing and toward sentimental ballads. Big band bookings declined as the costs of road trips rose and the bands began breaking up.

And the Swing Era, as such, was over. For a statement on what its passing meant to its most devout adherents we can turn again to Ralph Gleason: "Those were carefree days, golden days, sequestered days, and they cannot come again. No more would there be those white mess jackets and the potted palms. No longer those warm nights with white flannels and blue jackets at the Roton Point Casino in South Norwalk or the Ritz Ballroom in Bridgeport. No longer those lovely formal evenings at Glen Island or Frank Dailey's or the Essex House or the Waldorf.

"Funny how the music can still do it, though. The taste of the Scotch, the snarl of the waiter when you had only a buck left to tip him. The fragrance of the girls in their summer dresses at the roadhouses. And all those nights listening to the radio. In the darkened living room, carried by your imagination to the College Inn, the Madhattan Room, the Garden Court in Berkeley, the Palladium, San Francisco's Peacock Court. The less cynical among us would actually breathe, 'They're playing our song.' Ah, yes. They played it for years, take your choice. It was any of hundreds, and they were all, all of them, such lovely melodies."

—JOHN STANTON

In this recent photograph there are no ghosts of boys in white dinner jackets and girls in filmy organdy dresses. But at the Swing Era's height, musicians and dancers at Glen Island Casino looked out from the ballroom over this balcony rail and the fieldstone seawall at the moon-burnished water of Long Island Sound and Fort Slocum's lights twinkling magically in the distance.

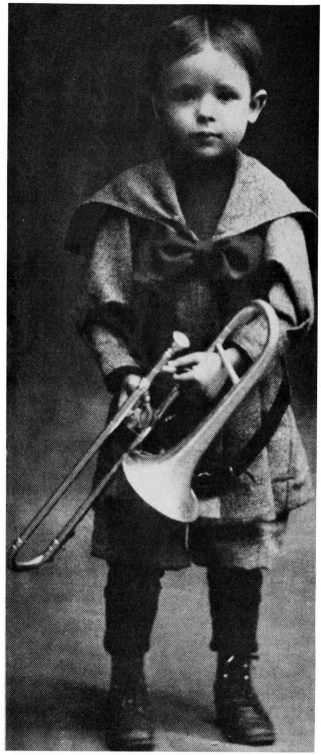

While still in transition from skirts to pants, Jimmy Dorsey *(above)* was a slide cornetist at age five. By seven he was playing with a band in Shenandoah, Pa. Younger brother Tommy also began on cornet, but by nine *(left)* he was a skilled trombonist. Taught by their coal-miner father, both boys could double on most brass and reed instruments.

The Men Who Made the Music:
The Dorsey Brothers

The first thing about the Dorseys was that they were Irish. They had Irish eyes and Irish smiles, Irish brooding moods and—notoriously—Irish tempers, mostly derived, I guess, from Tess Dorsey, the stout and sentimental mother who gave birth to James Francis on Leap Year's Day of 1904 and to Thomas Francis 21 months later. Their musicianship was the bequest of their father Thomas, a thin and professorial man wildly miscast in his job as a $10.20-a-week coal miner in Shenandoah, Pennsylvania. For extra earnings father Dorsey gave music lessons and coached bands. From about the time they started school, his sons got cornet lessons from their old man, who then veered them to sax and trombone. "I want my lads to go somewhere," he insisted. "They got me to teach them, and I didn't have nobody."

In their early teens the Dorsey boys were already in their father's band, playing waltzes and two-steps and quadrilles. Only Jimmy went to high school briefly. When they were 16 and 18, the Dorseys enlisted some other teen-agers into an orchestra, euphorically dubbed the Wild Canaries, and played a summer at Carlin's amusement park in Baltimore. A couple of years later Jimmy signed on with Jean Goldkette's jazz band in Detroit and got Goldkette to hire Tommy. Goldkette's cornetist in those years was Bix Beiderbecke, as instructive a jazz player as the Dorseys could possibly have known in their musical development. From Goldkette's incubator they went on, one or the other or both, to most of the big bands of the '20s, Paul Whiteman, Vincent Lopez, Rudy Vallee, Red Nichols, Roger Wolf Kahn—one-night stands, recording sessions, radio shows. A payroll voucher for the Paul Whiteman band in 1928 shows Jimmy Dorsey making $200 a week, $50 more than Bing Crosby and plenty of scratch for those days.

By then Jimmy Dorsey was a master technician of the alto saxophone. A textbook he wrote, with its exercises and advice to aspiring musicians, became the standard for anyone who wanted to play alto sax in a dance band. With Whiteman, he was featured as a virtuoso, and his specialty, later recorded as *Oodles of Noodles*, became the basis for his theme, *Contrasts*, as well as *Tailspin*.

Influential as Jimmy was as a jazz soloist, Tommy on trombone topped his brother as a pop instrumentalist and probably affected the course of popular music more. In the late '30s and early '40s it used to startle traditional jazz fans to find out that the veteran New Orleans trombonist, Kid Ory, who had played with King Oliver and had given Louis Armstrong his first job, insisted that his favorite trombone player was Tommy Dorsey.

During the early '30s the Dorseys headquartered in New York. They were in constant demand for studio work, for not only could they solo, but also they were schooled, reading musicians who were, like their father, perfectionists. Both were in the bands of many of the top radio programs. They played a lot with Glenn Miller, so it was a natural thing that Miller, admiring the Dorseys and not yet ready to become a band leader himself, should urge the former leaders of the Wild Canaries to start their own big band. Years later Jimmy Dorsey flatly stated that "the instigator of the band was none other than Glenn Miller."

Glen Gray had already discovered a market among young people for a white band that played something that might be equated with the style of the big Negro dance bands, Fletcher Henderson's, Jimmie Lunceford's, Duke Ellington's and McKinney's Cotton Pickers of Don Redman. Gray had been a smash success at Glen Island Casino and in ballrooms across the country, and it seemed possible

Thomas Dorsey Sr. hid his sons' shoes to keep the boys home practicing. If their progress, reviewed nightly, failed to please him, he knew his wife had let them out. Finally satisfied with their achievements, he said proudly, "I can't be playin' with my sons any more. They're gettin' too fast."

that all dance music need not necessarily be limited to the sweet, bland, lushly orchestrated music of leaders like Guy Lombardo, Vincent Lopez and Eddy Duchin.

The Dorseys' unofficial headquarters in the mid-'30s was a saloon called Plunkett's, strategically located on 53rd Street. The two brothers, and the rest of the studio men with jazz leanings, could hang out there and make their radio shows on time. To Plunkett's in 1933 came members of the old Smith Ballew band, stranded by a canceled date and introduced by Glenn Miller, who had been Ballew's trombonist, arranger and manager. Jimmy and Tommy began to make their first records with "The Dorsey Brothers" on the label, though the band was hardly more than a pickup group. (For one recording, the bandleader was neither Jimmy nor Tommy but a musician fated for a different kind of fame, Eugene Ormandy, who wound up as musical director of the Philadelphia Orchestra.) Later, recruiting sidemen from among the clientele at Plunkett's, they began assembling a big band and building a reputation on records. They did a lot of accompaniment work: among those they played for were Mildred Bailey, the Boswell Sisters and Bing Crosby. Tightening and perfecting their organization, they put out a long stream of discs for Decca in 1934. They also played dates up and down the East Coast, and in the spring of 1935 settled down in Glen Island Casino for what they hoped would be their lucky break into radio.

The band was a stunning, instant hit. Even the senior Dorsey, ear to loudspeaker back in Shenandoah, remarked judiciously, "The boys are getting so they execute better all the time."

Just so. But all through the years that they had been perfecting themselves as jazz-swing musicians, the Dorseys had also been honing another talent—for combat. Mother Tess Dorsey recalled that "there was always this bickerin' between them. Tommy was a great one for pushin', and Jimmy for takin' his own sweet time." The hot-tempered, whisky-drinking brothers themselves never troubled to deny their rivalry, perhaps because they knew that underneath it lay respect and loyalty. When they were apart, each always referred to the other as "The Brother."

Fistfulls of brotherly love

Their fights, and they were authentic fistfights, were no doubt part of a natural tendency to get their Irish up, and this penchant led them into celebrated scraps with others as well as one another. Music stands bore the main brunt of a tiff Tommy once had with Benny Goodman, but on another occasion actor Jon Hall emerged from Tommy's house with cuts and contusions requiring 50 stitches. Benny Goodman has recalled that Jimmy left the Ted Lewis band after a New Year's Eve argument which ended with Jimmy's belting Lewis over the head with a clarinet. "It seems that everybody had a few drinks and was feeling good, and Jimmy decided that was a fine time to panic the folks at the club with an imitation of Lewis playing clarinet." As late as 1949, Jimmy, annoyed by a heckling milkman at a dance, clubbed the fellow with a clarinet, raising a two-inch lump.

Of Tommy's temper, arranger Sy Oliver says, "He had a temper all right but it was usually in a good cause. He got in more trouble trying to help other people than anything else. He wasn't the kind of guy who would start

JD (*second from left*) and TD (*right*) pose with other members of the Wild Canaries (their first band) in 1922 when they played at Carlin's, an amusement park in Baltimore.

Tommy beat bandleader Charlie Barnet at tic-tac-toe on the set of *A Song Is Born* in which both played their horns. Danny Kaye and Benny Goodman had speaking parts.

Tommy clowns for a home movie. From left are: Frank Devol, Yvonne King, Jack Egan, Tommy, Alyce King and Dick Morgan. All but Egan, a press agent, were with Horace Heidt.

Beneath the hostilities of the battling Dorseys lay a deep mutual affection which showed itself oftener with the passing of the years, as in this moment at a late '30s ballgame.

a fight with a waiter—he'd start a fight with the manager."

The intra-Dorsey feuding was "mainly about music," Jimmy noted. "In our short-pants days, the battles concerned who played cornet better." Tommy recalled that he "got so mad at Jimmy one day that I went over to his room and smashed all of his saxophones on the radiator. Once, in a surge of brotherly affection, I went down to the pier to meet Jimmy on the *Ile de France*. Jimmy had been touring Europe in an orchestra that included Muggsy Spanier and George Brunies. We hadn't seen each other for months, but within five minutes we were fighting again." Yet Howard Christianson, who was a friend of both Dorseys and later Jimmy's manager, diagnosed their relationship as "squabbles that may have seemed bitter" overlying "a basic foundation of love."

A tempo tantrum, a sizzling split

One of their battles was over Tommy's preference for a fast beat over Jimmy's preference for a slow one. And it was just that question that took the Dorsey feud to the flash point on the night of May 30, 1935.

The band was about to play *I'll Never Say Never Again Again*, and Tommy kicked off the tempo. Jimmy looked up from his seat and slyly remarked, "Isn't that a little too fast, Mac?" Tommy put down the trombone, walked off the bandstand, drove to New York and never looked back. From then on for years, people had to talk less about "the Dorseys" and more about "JD" and "TD." JD kept the band, and even the name "Dorsey Brothers" for the rest of that gig at Glen Island and the rest of the Decca recording contract. TD went out on his own.

It is interesting now to go back and see how the jazz world, where both Dorseys had strong reputations and where their hearts were really at, treated them. Everybody dug the Dorsey Brothers band. It swung, for one thing, as few other big white bands had swung, and it had shown, on records and then on grinding night-after-night road tours, that it was possible to make some silly Tin Pan Alley songs swing and give the soloists room to blow jazz.

So when the Brothers broke apart, the hot music fans split down the middle. Some of them said that Jimmy kept a jazz-oriented band and Tommy went commercial. Just as many said exactly the opposite. I remember once listening to Tommy Dorsey records with Artie Shaw when a woman who was with us sneered at Tommy's "commercialism." I thought Artie was going to hit her, even though, as it happened, the woman was his current wife. Like the rest of TD's peers, Artie Shaw knew that Tommy was a hard worker and a superb musician with a dedication to what was musically right.

In hindsight, with the Dorseys established by history in the top ranks of swing, it is easy to make the judgment: the Dorseys had perfect taste hooked to high talents and arduous schooling to produce impeccable artistry. If this carried them, a decade after their split, to grosses running from $625,000 to $991,000 a year, and to lifetime earnings high in the millions, that seems more like just reward than the consequence of pandering to the public. Their scores and scores of lovely classics show that their real dedication was to their art and not to money. Tommy got rich enough to buy Walter Chrysler Jr.'s yacht (which he renamed *The*

Sentimentalist), but his passion was music, not yachting.

I remember Tommy standing up there on the bandstand with that sharp nose and those bookkeeper's glasses and a suit that looked as though it didn't fit. Years later, when Tommy was a millionaire, his suits still looked as though they didn't fit. Jimmy always looked as if his clothes had been not only tailored but possibly woven for him.

With the original band Jimmy went first to the West Coast for a long run on a commercial radio hour with Bing Crosby, and then to hit records: *All of Me* and *Six Lessons from Madame La Zonga* with Helen O'Connell singing; *I Get Along without You Very Well* with Bob Eberly; and a series of Eberly-O'Connell duets like *Green Eyes* and *Tangerine*. Jimmy's records with these two singers made his band one of the biggest draws in box-office history up to then.

Tommy had to find a band. He thought of Joe Haymes who was then at the McAlpin Hotel in Manhattan. Haymes was a leader who had a rather small name with the public but a good name among musicians for having interesting bands. Haymes never felt really comfortable as a leader, and Dorsey took over almost all of the band as his base, including Haymes's chief arranger, Paul Weston. TD signed a contract with RCA Victor and began recording in the fall of 1935;

Victor already had Benny Goodman under contract and had discovered that the swingy music everybody was hearing on radio could sell discs. Tommy whipped the band into shape with the perfectionism that his bitterest enemies always had to concede. Howard Christianson remembers that Tommy would "get up in the middle of the night to get things done—he was a tireless worker." The first thing Tommy did was to stick Sterling Bose in the trumpet section. "Bozo" was a Beiderbecke devotee who played with a driving, rhythmic style of his own, and Tommy chose him out of conviction that the brass section should have a standout jazz trumpet soloist. Tommy's brass section always had top soloists and he always gave them room, just as Jimmy's saxophone sections were distinguished for team play.

Then Tommy added the first of two men in a rhythm section that was to make swing history. Dave Tough, a tiny, mournful-looking man who resembled a jockey, came originally from Chicago. Tommy heard Dave the first time, Dave later recalled, one day when Tough was practicing in a back room at Plunkett's. Tough was an epileptic and a problem drinker, but in 1936 he had sobered up temporarily and Tommy went looking for him for the band, eventually driving to Boston to find him working in some joint. The next recruit was a guitarist who was then play-

Danny Kaye mimes a solo for *A Song is Born*. Band includes (from left) Louis Armstrong, Lionel Hampton, Dorsey, Goodman and Barnet. TD and BG squared off at one session but, Barnet says, knocked down only music stands.

JD and his clarinet head a wedge of bandsmen in the 1944 MGM opus, *Lost in a Harem*, starring Abbott and Costello as oriental magicians. Jimmy and his boys blew in occasionally with appropriate music like Jimmy's own *John Silver*.

ing on 52nd Street in the Hickory House, with Wingy Manone's group. He was Carmen Mastren, a young player unknown aside from his appearance at the Hickory House, where Tommy sat in now and then.

For other trumpets Tommy got Andy Ferretti and Bill Graham and, later, Max Kaminsky and Peewee Erwin. Bud Freeman, the Chicago tenor sax player, came in, and by the middle of 1936 TD had the kind of band he wanted, except that he had not yet enlisted Bunny Berigan for a solo trumpet chair. Bunny joined briefly, left to lead his own band and came back three years later. The things he recorded with TD, *Marie* and *Song of India* especially, are among the finest examples of the Berigan style.

Looking back, it is obvious that Tommy Dorsey loved the Chicago-style Dixieland musicians. Carmen Mastren was working with a Dixie combo when Tommy hired him, and Freeman was lengendary as a hot soloist. Thus Tommy shaped a band that could transform itself in an instant from a big swing band into the Dixieland combination that he called the Clambake Seven, including his own trombone, one of his trumpet soloists, Freeman on tenor, a clarinet, plus a rhythm section. Joe Dixon was Tommy's first clarinetist; Johnny Mince lasted the longest. Since TD played pretty fair tailgate when he wanted to, and he had a tight but swinging rhythm section, it was a

winning combination on numbers like *The Music Goes Round and Round*. The big band/small group adaptability put TD right in there with the man he saw as his only rival, Benny Goodman.

Tommy used his players with skill. Dixon and Mince were expert clarinetists, influenced by the same early jazzmen as had influenced Goodman, but Tommy conceded the clarinet to Goodman and used them sparingly, usually for fills and short choruses. For his long swinging solos he leaned on two instruments. One was the swing tenor of Bud Freeman, and then of Bud's successors—Babe Russin, Don Lodice, Skeets Herfurt, Boomie Richman and, very briefly, Paul Gonsalves of Duke Ellington's band. The other instrument was the trumpet, played at times by Bunny Berigan, Peewee Erwin, Sterling Bose, Max Kaminsky, Lee Castle, Ziggy Elman and others. When the mood was right, Tommy would let them stretch the arrangement, usually the roughly three minutes of a 78 rpm disc, by playing chorus after chorus until the crowd was screaming.

The Jimmy Dorsey band, as the successor to the original Dorsey Brothers aggregation and composed of all-star studio men, stressed ensemble. Fewer JD sidemen in the late '30s had the stature of such TD jazz players as Bunny Berigan, Bud Freeman or Davey Tough. But they could all play, and they played together with beautiful precision.

Tommy listens to a record with his first wife, Mildred ("Toots"), and their children, Pat and Thomas III (now an IBM executive). At his big New Jersey house, Tommy entertained lavishly, bringing home carloads of weekend guests.

In 1944, Tommy and his second wife, actress Pat Dane, were in court, accused of assaulting actor Jon Hall, who, Tommy said, had tried to embrace Pat. The case was dismissed.

On Thanksgiving Day, 1951, Tommy, his third wife, Jane, and their daughter Susan posed with a turkey—to plug an airline catering firm—before a band tour of Brazil which was cut short by disputes with impresarios and ended in litigation.

Both Dorseys scored with what the music business used to call novelties, and with vocalists. Tommy's record of *Boogie Woogie* was one of RCA Victor's best sellers for years, and Jimmy made a whole series of novelty and jazz instrumentals for Decca that were prime jukebox favorites. To sing, Tommy had Edythe Wright, a thin and sexy-sounding girl who made, among other numbers, *You Must Have Been a Beautiful Baby, Dipsy Doodle* and *Music Maestro Please.* For some of his most memorable hits—*Marie, Yearning,* and *Who*—Tommy used Jack Leonard, with the band acting as a chorus responding to him. Comic as it seems now, TD's swing versions of Rimsky-Korsakoff's *Song of India* and Mendelssohn's *Spring Song* earned anguished accusations of desecration from many solemn admirers of the classics. "What's the harm in giving these old masters a coat of 1935 enamel?" Tommy joked.

Jimmy hit big box-office successes in theaters and ballrooms and within a few years gained added strength from the duo-vocals of Helen O'Connell and Bob Eberly.

And then, of course, after Jack Leonard left Tommy (first to go on his own, unsuccessfully, and then to go into the army), TD ultimately picked up a skinny kid from the Harry James band, Frank Sinatra. It was a break for both of them. Sinatra learned from Dorsey as well as contributing some of the most successful moments the TD band ever had. Frank candidly says that his style, which became *the* style for ballad singers, evolved from the way Tommy played trombone. Tommy had an amazing consistency of tone and the ability to extend the sound for long periods without seeming to breathe. Sinatra picked that up. "Tommy taught me everything I knew about singing," Frank has said. "He was my real education. In the middle of a phrase, while the tone was still being carried through the trombone, he'd take a quick breath and play another four bars."

Jo Stafford, who did *Embraceable You, Who Can I Turn To* and other numbers with Tommy, said almost the same thing. "I'm certain that Tommy's trombone style must have had an effect on every singer who worked with the band. I know that in my case I learned a great deal about phrasing and breath control while sitting on the bandstand listening to him play."

Although both brothers were fans of the big black bands such as Duke Ellington and Count Basie, Tommy adopted more of their ideas than Jimmy did, and even, when he hired Sy Oliver from Jimmie Lunceford and later Ernie Wilkins from Basie, moved directly into their style. Tommy offered Oliver $5,000 more than "whatever you're making, playing and writing for Jimmie," and Oliver went on to write many famous and popular originals and arrangements for TD, including *Opus One, On the Sunny Side of the Street* and *Well, Git It!*

"He was great to work for," says Sy. "He gave me a completely free hand. He modeled the band on what I was doing. He never even assigned the vocals." At a time when Dorsey had Frank Sinatra, Jo Stafford and the Pied Pipers singing for him, he would let Sy decide who sang what in an Oliver arrangement. Sy left Tommy in 1943 only because he was drafted. By that time he thought the band was "one of the best bands I'd ever worked with."

Tommy paid his musicians well, but he wasn't as open-handed as Paul Whiteman had been. In the late '30s he hired the sharp little pianist Joe Bushkin, after Joe sat in on trumpet (on which he doubled occasionally) one night with TD's band at Frank Dailey's Meadowbrook in New Jersey. Bushkin had played with Wingy Manone, Joe

Jane, Jimmy's wife for 21 years, divorced him. The grounds: habitually waking her before dawn to listen to his recordings.

Marsala, Eddie Condon and other 52nd Street bands. Bushkin's description of the hiring: "Tommy asked how much I was making with Bunny Berigan and I said 'Ninety dollars,' and that was it." Bushkin wrote several hit-list songs, such as *Oh Look at Me Now.* By a happy chance, he soloed on celesta in *I'll Never Smile Again,* just because there happened to be a celesta in the recording studio.

During World War II both Dorseys played frequently at Army camps, Navy bases, hospitals and war-bond rallies. Tommy survived the war years well with theater and location jobs that people could get to despite gasoline rationing, and came out with a box-office rating that was still tops. But Jimmy suffered irreparable losses when, after their series of hit discs, Helen O'Connell left him to get married, and Bob Eberly went into the Army. The band lost commercial appeal, but Jimmy continued to play a lot of punchy jazz for one-nighters and hotels.

Jimmy, who never had Tommy's hard edge, did not fight the decline. Friends have always insisted that if Tommy had not quit that night in Glen Island, Jimmy would really have been content to sit in the saxophone section forever and just play. Everybody who ever worked for Jimmy loved him. He was gentle and kind and generous. He put up with drunkenness and missed rehearsals that Tommy, whom some bandsmen remember as "cruel" and "ruthless" and even "brutal," would never have tolerated. And Jimmy had his moments of box-office glory, too. One time in 1940, a Texas oilman flew Jimmy's band to Houston in two chartered planes for a birthday party at a one-performance cost of $10,000. His postwar slump can probably be traced partly to bitter episodes in his personal life—his house burned down, he quarreled with his wife, and one of his managers stole a lot of money.

Tommy, who fought the world as vigorously as he fought Jimmy, battled his booking agencies and eventually, when his contract expired, took out a full-page advertisement in *Billboard* announcing his "escape" and the formation of his own agency. Angered at the prices he was getting from ballrooms for his band, he headed several

On November 19, 1956, the Dorsey brothers and their 82-year-old mother celebrated Tommy's 51st birthday at the Hotel Statler in New York. A week later Tommy was dead.

PHEW!

After 15 Years I am finally
out of the clutches of . . . . .
YOU KNOW WHO!!!

I am being Booked exclusively by . . .
TOMDOR ENTERPRISES, Inc.
1619 Broadway • CIrcle 6-4865 • New York 19, N. Y.
for all available dates, please contact the above.

Tommy Dorsey

Personal Management
PERSONAL MANAGEMENT, Inc.
1619 Broadway • JU 6-4495 • New York 19, N. Y.

DECCA
RECORDS

When his MCA contract expired, Tommy ran this ad in
Billboard announcing his own "Tomdor" management.

other bandleaders in buying the Casino Gardens in suburban Los Angeles. One Saturday night Tommy coolly an-
nounced at the Palladium that on the following weekend
he would be playing at his own ballroom.

All through the late '30s the feud went on strenuously,
each Dorsey band striving to top the other in record sales,
hit tunes and theater grosses. Sometimes they played eyeball to eyeball in the same city, and when the Dorseys
met they gave one another thin smiles and barely cordial
salutations. Once they scheduled a let's-make-up meeting
at the Astor Hotel in Manhattan, where Tommy had just
added violins to his band. Jimmy, full of booze, couldn't
resist saying sarcastically that Tommy *needed* violins. So
Tommy jumped down from the bandstand and socked
Jimmy. Their reconciliation began at their father's funeral
in 1942, and they began to work amicably, together.

Christianson recalls that once "when Jimmy was ill in
Philadelphia, Tommy rode a train nightly from New York
to head the band." When they joined to go into the sheet-
music business, they smoothly solved the problem of hier-
archy by getting two sets of business cards, one that said,
"Jimmy Dorsey, President" and another that said, "Tommy
Dorsey, President." This business collaboration outmoded
one aggravation of their rivalry: the heightening of it by
their managers for box-office and publicity value. They
found another common interest in making *The Fabulous
Dorseys,* a rosy-hued 1947 movie depicting their climb to
success from the Pennsylvania coal mines. Tommy (but
not Jimmy) was practically on the wagon from 1937 to
1940, removing one detonator of Dorsey battles

Ultimately their musical disagreements faded and their
perennial mutual respect came to dominate. One day
Tommy was kicking around some TV show ideas with

Soon after announcing that they would join forces, the Dorseys appeared as guest sidemen with Ray Anthony at Duke
University's "Joe College Weekend." With this happy 1953
tryout began their three final, and successful, years together.

Jackie Gleason and heard himself say, "What about my
brother Jimmy?" And so in 1953 Jimmy and three remnant
members of his band joined Tommy's band, 18 years after
the walkout at Glen Island. But it wasn't the Dorsey Brothers band this time. It was Tommy's band, the Tommy
Dorsey orchestra featuring Jimmy Dorsey, at Manhattan's
Hotel Statler. The band would play a set with Jimmy's
arrangements featuring Jimmy, and the two brothers would
play a couple of numbers together. It worked out well—so
well, in fact, that they went on the CBS television network
(forgetting Tommy's earlier fulminations against the
ravages of TV in the entertainment world) as a summer
replacement for the Jackie Gleason show.

They clicked, and in passing—this must have some socio-
logical significance—introduced Elvis Presley to the general American audience. Their success induced Gleason to
splice the Dorsey program into his regular CBS series.
Tommy and Jimmy continued to work together, and in the
fall of 1956 Tommy returned to the Statler in New York
and worked out of there for one-nighters and college proms.

Tommy's married life had been stormy enough to have
cracked up in two divorces, and that fall, at the age of 51,
he was nearing a third. One night at his 14-room house
in Greenwich, Connecticut, he ate a heavy meal of Italian
food sent up from New York. His wife, Jane New Dorsey,
a onetime Copacabana showgirl, and her mother dined
with him, and the occasion was apparently not too frigid
even though Jane was sueing Tommy for a split on grounds
of "intolerable cruelty." He went to his room at nine o'clock
and locked the door in deference to the terms of the
separation required for the divorce. When he had not
reappeared at two o'clock the next afternoon, his wife got
Tommy's business manager, Vincent Carbone, to climb
through the bedroom window. Tommy was dead, suf-
focated, doctors found, on food regurgitated while he was
asleep. He had taken a lot of sleeping tablets, not, it
seemed an intentionally lethal amount, but enough, probably, to have kept him from coping with the nausea. He
left a bitter note, not of suicide but of protest against the
divorce. At the funeral in Manhattan, an organist played
Tommy's ever-so-familiar theme, *I'm Gettin' Sentimental
over You,* and Louis Armstrong sent a wreath woven
around a trombone.

Jimmy carried on for a few months, ironically scoring
his biggest record hit. He had recorded, under his own
name for Fraternity Records, an arrangement of an old
ballad called *So Rare,* with something of a rock 'n' roll
beat to it, and Jimmy's alto on the pretty tune. Just as he
was about to be awarded a gold record for its sales, and
only seven months after Tommy's death, Jimmy died of
lung cancer. Just 22 years after that Glen Island contract
they were both gone.

Isn't that a little too fast, Mac?

—RALPH J. GLEASON

The Men Who Made the Music:
Bob Crosby

For some seven years of the Swing Era, Bob Crosby and his orchestra ripsnorted across the land, delighting multitudes from real Dixieland fans who loved the solid music to squarer types who liked the leader's engaging manner, casual chatter and pleasant singing. Few listeners knew that the leader could play only the most rudimentary drum.

The band had some of the greatest blowers of the age and enough arranging and composing talent to stock three ordinary bands. They were purveyors of the New Orleans style of 30 or 40 years earlier, not of the new "swing" of pacesetters like Benny Goodman, Glenn Miller and the Dorsey Brothers. But instead of being treated like anachronisms they stayed at or near the top of the polls for most of those seven years with Benny and Glenn and Tommy and Jimmy. The sidemen drew better salaries than most did in those days. The band broadcast regularly from the best night spots. New York's Lexington and New Yorker hotels, Chicago's Congress Hotel and Blackhawk Restaurant, Boston's Ritz-Carlton Hotel and the Palomar Ballroom in Los Angeles. They made movies—*Let's Make Music, Presenting Lily Mars, Thousands Cheer, See Here, Private Hargrove* and *Rookies on Parade.*

At one time the band was trailed everywhere by a friend of one of the sidemen. She was Mrs. Celeste LeBrosi, a wealthy Long Island widow right out of Scott Fitzgerald, who traveled in a limousine equipped with a two-wheeled trailer for her luggage. When the band was at the Ritz-Carlton, she took the hotel's whole top floor and ran up an entertainment tab of more than $1,100 in a single week.

The Bob Crosby band began early in 1935 with eight musicians in search of a leader. They were all refugees from one of the bands of Ben Pollack, the gifted drummer whose various sidemen over the years could stock a swinging hall of fame. This particular band broke up in California because the musicians were becoming discouraged. Business in those Depression days was poor, the sidemen's salaries had been cut and, as trumpeter Yank Lawson says, "Future bookings didn't look bright. We started having meetings and talking about an alternative." Bassist Harry Goodman went off to join his brother Benny, but most of the sidemen, including Lawson, clarinetist-arranger Matty Matlock, saxophonist Eddie Miller, trumpeter Charlie Spivak, pianist Gil Bowers, guitarist Nappy Lamare, drummer Ray Bauduc and saxo-

Gathered in, on and around a 1935 Dodge convertible coupé are the original members of what became one of the era's happiest bands. Bob Crosby is at the wheel, beside drummer Ray Bauduc. In the back row: Joe Harris (trombone), Charlie

phonist-organizer Gil Rodin, decided to form a new band under the direction of trombonist Jack Teagarden, who had left Pollock a little earlier.

They made their various ways to New York where Rodin, who had landed a radio job with Benny Goodman, kept them alive with occasional one-night stands. They also cut some records under the name of Clark Randall and His Orchestra. "Randall" was Frank Tennille who had been a featured vocalist with Pollack and whom the sidemen chose as the new band's first front man. Those Brunswick sides, made in March 1935, are collectors' items now because the line-up is virtually the same as that of the first Bob Crosby Orchestra and because they had an extra trombonist named Glenn Miller who later decided to go off with Ray Noble instead of with the Bobcats.

In January 1935 "Pollack's Orphans," as other musicians called them, got a break. Rodin, as contractor for a new radio show, Kellogg's College Prom with Red Nichols, found berths in the band for some of his friends. The Nichols band soon caught the ear of Tommy Rockwell of the Rockwell-O'Keefe agency, then one of the biggest bookers and builders of bands. But to go on their own, the Orphans needed a personable front man with a well-known name. Tennille, who agreed to step aside, was not famous. Teagarden, the band's next choice, was under contract to Paul Whiteman. None of the sidemen could wave a baton convincingly, not even Rodin, a fine organizer who had brought Goodman, Miller and Teagarden into Pollack's band.

Cork O'Keefe, the other half of Rockwell-O'Keefe, offered the band a choice of three batonists: singing trumpeter

Green (violin), Phil Hart (trumpet), Eddie Bergman (violin), Yank Lawson (trumpet), Bob Haggart (bass), Deane Kincaide (arranger-saxophone). In front: Matty Matlock (clarinet), Gil Bowers (piano), Eddie Miller (saxophone),

Frank Tennille (vocalist), Gil Rodin (manager-saxophone), Nappy Lamare (guitar). Horns soon replaced the fiddlers. Some others also left, but Rodin, Bauduc, Haggart, Lamare, Miller, Lawson and Matlock were with Crosby at the end.

were jazz-mad gypsies, roaming the country to play dance halls, picnics, carnivals and cabarets."

To Bob Crosby at age 21 the Orphans' offer seemed heaven-sent. Youngest of an expansive Irish household of seven children, he was born on August 25, 1913 in Spokane, Washington. Bob played baseball and football and was Spokane High's tennis champion in 1929.

Like brother Bing, who was a little more than nine years his senior, Bob attended Gonzaga University and like Bing left college for show business. He tried to make it Bing's way—by singing. He attempted a debut in an amateur show at 13. The organist played a lead-in to *Five Foot Two Eyes Of Blue* five times; Bob opened his mouth five times but nothing came out, and finally he fled.

The shadow of the 'best' Crosby

He did better singing at a walkathon. A Spokane radio station did a weekly on-scene broadcast of the endurance contest and bandleader Anson Weeks heard the station in San Francisco. "Anson knew that Bing had a brother who also sang," Bob said later, "so he sent for me. I was picking cucumbers in Spokane when I got the call." Bob responded to Anson's call so eagerly that he forgot to pack his suspenders and sang his first date with his arms clamped tightly to his sides to keep his pants up. Weeks sent him home after six weeks but eventually rehired him and Bob sang with the band for two years. Then in 1934 came an offer to sing with the Dorsey Brothers band. Tommy, Bob recalls somewhat bitterly, was less than enthusiastic. "Tommy wouldn't let me sing for two nights. He said, 'I got the best band in the land. Why can't I have the best Crosby?'" Tommy soon modulated into a brighter view of Bob and in his six months with the Dorseys Bob sang often and made more than 30 records with the band. But Bob saw only a limited future for himself as a boy singer. He wanted a more active role.

All his life Bob Crosby has fought to stand outside the shadow of "the best Crosby." His father, Harry Lillis Crosby Sr., and his other brothers, Larry, Everett and Ted, all seemed content with niches in Bing's enterprises. Bob and Bing never battled like the Dorseys; Bing often helped his younger brother, sometimes surreptitiously, and Bob developed a line of jokes about Bing. "What? Fight with the Bank of America?" he once said when asked if he quarreled with Bing. "I was 14 before I knew Bing was my brother and not my father. Bing sent me his old clothes. . . . I was the only kid in the first grade who had tux pants with pleats. . . . We are blood relations but his blood is richer than mine. . . . I once found a $5 bill. I took it to Bing. He said, 'We have to share it.' He took it to the drugstore to change. He kept three, gave me two. That's the story of my life."

Just before he joined Pollack's Orphans, Bob was singing at the Paramount Theater with Lee Wiley, already a great song stylist. "As comedy, it would have been terrific," he said later with disarming modesty, "but it was meant to be romantic." Bob suffered from no illusions about his musical ability but worked hard to improve his voice; for a time he even took lessons from retired opera diva Amelita Galli-Curci. He had charm, a quick wit, an ability to get along with people and a passion to make his own way. Fronting a band seemed a good chance. "Nobody could say Bing was a better bandleader than me because he didn't lead a band."

Bob spent his 14th summer picking cucumbers near Spokane. His father, a pickle factory's bookkeeper, got him the job.

Johnny ("Scat") Davis, Goldie (the sole professional name of Harry Goldfield then playing trumpet and doing a tap dance for Paul Whiteman) and Bing Crosby's kid brother, George Robert Crosby, better known as Bob, recently boy singer for the Dorsey brothers.

Rodin and his friends decided that the band was already loaded with featured instrumentalists, that Davis and Goldie were a bit too corny and that Bob would do because he was, as Lawson says, "Bing's brother and a good-looking guy who would make a good front. And we figured, if he was good enough to sing with the Dorsey brothers he couldn't be too bad in that department." Lawson and the others also liked, and still do, Bob's easygoing ways and unpretentious charm.

Crosby and the Orphans decided to go it together while "sippin' sodas" in a drugstore on 55th Street and Sixth Avenue. They became the "Bob Crosby–Gil Rodin Corporation," chartered in the state of New York and billed professionally as Bob Crosby and his Orchestra, though more widely known as the Bobcats, a name which technically applied only to the small jazz combo within the band.

"During the next seven years," Crosby said later, "we

Bob's debut with the band was a hastily arranged one-nighter at the Roseland Ballroom. "After an hour on that stand," Rodin recalled, "with Bob out front wisecracking and waving his magic wand, we knew we had our man." Bob's breezy charm added a personal identity to the band's strong musical identity, while Rodin attended to hiring, firing, rehearsing, and planning programs as well as buying and writing arrangements. One girl singer might complain that Bob kept the best songs for himself, as singing bandleaders often did; more important to the sidemen were Crosby's frequent public mentions of each of them, keeping listeners aware of each man's individual contribution. Nobody left the band just because he couldn't stand Bob, and years later many gladly came back and toured with him again.

Bob had executive skills, too. In 1940 the band arrived at the financially ailing Empire Theater in Syracuse, New York, to find the house dark and the manager missing. Crosby rounded up electricians, stage hands, ushers, box office attendants and union officials, generating so much publicity in the process that the band played to record-breaking attendance.

From 1935 to 1942 the Crosby band won fame as a versatile outfit whose theme song was Gershwin's gentle *Summertime* and whose repertory included hit ballads and jump tunes, novelty and comedy numbers and even waltzes. But its musicians found their true inspiration in the collective improvisations of the band's "danceable Dixieland."

The key sidemen were dedicated to good jazz. Drummer Ray Bauduc, tenor saxist Eddie Miller and guitarist-singer Nappy Lamare were natives of New Orleans and had been raised on the righteous sounds. The biggest problem with Bauduc, says Rodin, was getting him to play dance music

in addition to Dixieland. "When we played ballads," Lawson says, "Bauduc was always fixing his drums."

Matty Matlock, born in Paducah, Kentucky, and raised in Nashville, played New Orleans-style clarinet and could score the classic jazz repertory for big band instrumentation without losing the essential spirit of the music. Bob Haggart, another great arranger, was born in Douglaston, Long Island—hardly a jazz mecca. But he quickly learned the New Orleans message from Bauduc and conveyed it both on his bass fiddle and on paper. The sidemen cheered him after playing through his first chart and remained his fervent fans. "He was one of the greatest talents in America," says Rodin, "and could have been one of the greatest writers in the world."

Deane Kincaide added another valuable arranging talent to the band, and Yank Lawson's driving trumpet, in the opinion of some listeners, helped sustain Bauduc's beat. Gil Rodin, the band's musical director, mentor, father-confessor and policy maker grew up in Chicago on hot music and was firmly committed to its virtues.

These men set the style and direction the band maintained through subsequent changes in personnel, especially in the piano, which the band called the "hex seat." Illness forced out Gil Bowers, the original pianist. The famous Joe Sullivan, who followed Bowers, wowed the band with his inspirational playing and contributed to its library such originals as *Little Rock Getaway* and *Gin Mill Blues*. Sullivan discovered he had tuberculosis when he had an injured arm X-rayed. The band played a big benefit for Joe and hired Bob Zurke as his replacement.

Zurke's small hands could not stretch to play the tenths required in stride piano style, but he compensated for this

In 1934, soon after some of its members posed for this baseball picture, the band of Ben Pollack *(fourth from left)* broke up in California. Gil Rodin *(in dark shirt, center)* later organized "Pollack's Orphans" into the Bob Crosby band.

Eddie Miller lifts a lissome leg as he joins Bob Haggart (center) and Nappy Lamare in one of the exhibitions which made the Crosby band a whole show in itself. The boys did their celebrated fan dance to the strains of *Beautiful Lady*.

with a dazzling contrapuntal technique. Someone in the band had to keep constant track of Zurke, a heavy drinker who once threatened to divorce his wife because she kept nothing in the refrigerator but food. When Zurke broke his leg, Pete Viera replaced him but soon developed arthritis. Sullivan returned briefly and finally Jess Stacy joined the band in 1939 and stayed to the end. Stacy had already made a name with Benny Goodman. "He was a little away from Dixieland," says Rodin, "a little more swing-oriented, but he adapted very well."

Among notable later recruits were trumpeter Billy Butterfield and a fat clarinetist, born Irving Prestopnik, who disliked the name "Irving" and had his name changed legally to just "Fazola." Everybody then called him Irving Fazola. Benny Goodman admired his big clarinet tone. "When you saw him without his clarinet," says Bob Haggart, "you wouldn't dream he could make such beautiful, sensitive sounds."

Because it was a corporation whose founding members split the profits every year, the Crosby band was more stable than most, but trouble developed when some felt the profits were too small. Part of the trouble, Gil Rodin says, was that Tom Rockwell had made himself a partner and took his profit off the top, charging the band for such things as part of the maintenance costs of his agency's New York office. In 1938 the band left Rockwell-O'Keefe for a rival agency, Music Corporation of America, and continued to operate as a cooperative, with highly beneficial financial results for members. In 1940 *Down Beat* published the following estimates of the members' incomes from the band: Crosby, $25,000; Rodin, $20,000; Bauduc, $17,000; Miller, Haggart and Lamare, $15,000 each; Matlock, $14,000; Butterfield, Stacy and Fazola, $10,000, and the other sidemen $8,000 each. These were good wages but few of the Cats were in it just for the money. "We didn't do it to be successful," says Rodin. "We did it to be happy."

Doris Day, one of the band's series of girl singers, who Crosby predicted would one day be a sensation, was paid at an annual rate of $3,000 during her brief tenure.

The Crosby band, unlike some big bands, usually featured a show of some kind. Tall Bob Haggart, flanked by Miller and Lamare, both short, all of them with their pant legs rolled to the knee, would perform a fan dance. Bauduc at the drums was a show all by himself, changing his approach to suit each soloist. He conserved his energy by sleeping a lot and could sleep anywhere he could find room to stretch out. Bauduc claimed he needed 12 hours to get eight hours' sleep because he "slept very slowly." At Chicago's Blackhawk Restaurant he and Haggart first improvised *Big Noise from Winnetka*. The simple but effective routine, still much in demand today, won the Crosby band a movie contract and a radio show.

Bob Ottum, a senior editor of *Sports Illustrated,* was in high school in Minneapolis when *Big Noise* first appeared.

"It introduced a fantastic new sound," he recalls, "back in the days before recording studio trickery and quadruple playbacks. Anyone listening to a record always knew who was playing what instrument. Then along came this special sort of *thumpy* sound full of delightful mystery because no one except those who had actually seen it performed knew how it was done.

"I first started hearing *Big Noise*—about 22 times a day —over station WCCO in Minneapolis and learned it was by Bob Haggart and Ray Bauduc who played bass and drums for Bob Crosby. I decided that either our family's old Philco radio was finally shot or that Haggart or Bauduc was first whistling and then chanting into a barrel. Our exclusive

North Side Jazz Symposium (about 11 of my Patrick Henry High School friends and one record player) decided Haggart was slapping his bass some new way. Then one wealthy club member who had been all the way to Chicago and attended one of the Sunday afternoon sessions by the Crosby band at the Blackhawk Restaurant revealed that 'Mister Bauduc takes his sticks, see, and taps them against the strings of the bass.' We called WCCO and got this flash out on the air the same night."

Haggart and Bauduc vividly recall the birth of *Big Noise.* The band played special Bobcat Fan Club gigs on Sundays at the Blackhawk, Bauduc remembers, and then did a radio broadcast from the restaurant. "All our fans came and packed the joint." One Sunday the band planned to record its broadcast, hoping the recordings would entice a big tobacco company into sponsoring the band. After the Fan Club show, ending with a session by the Bobcats, Crosby asked the crowd to let the sidemen rest a few minutes before the broadcast.

Nothing doing. "The kids held onto the rubber carpet that carried the drums," Bauduc says. "They were screaming and yelling for more." Crosby asked Bauduc and Haggart to distract the fans so the rest of the band could "catch their wind and rest their chops." The two began jamming and Bauduc noticed that the cold weather had tightened the head of his big floor tom-tom, bringing its pitch close to the open G-string of Haggart's bass.

Big Noise from Winnetka was another Crosby band act and became so popular that it was a feature of the band's first movie, *Let's Make Music (below)*. It was repeated in two other films, *Reveille with Beverly* and *Presenting Lily Mars.*

The band struck paydirt in 1938 at Chicago's Blackhawk Restaurant. On Sundays, as part of the act, the eight Bobcats would leave the bandstand and play on the dance floor, where the fans crowded around them, roaring approval.

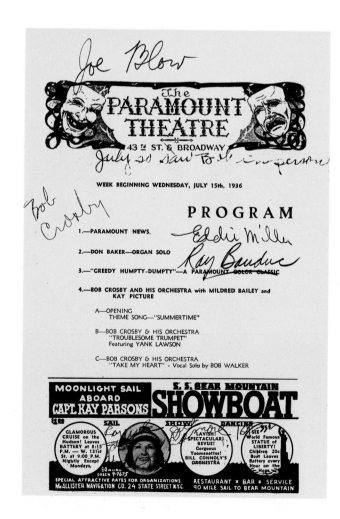

Jean Berger of New York, once vice president of the Bob Crosby fan club, still treasures these mementos: an autographed program ("Joe Blow" was Matty Matlock), a Bobcat tie clasp and a Bobcat Club membership certificate.

"So I started vamping on the tom-toms and Haggart on the bass," says Bauduc. "We went along for a while, then I said to Hag, 'Give with the whistle,' and he did."

"I have always been able to whistle through my teeth," says Haggart. "I'm not sure I can whistle the *other* way."

"I remember a gag I used to do with Nappy Lamare when we were kids," says Bauduc, "playing on his banjo with my drumsticks. So when Hag was through whistling I started vamping from tom-toms to the G-string with my sticks, and Hag, thinking quickly, started arpeggioing up and down on the G-string. The kids were screaming. We really broke it up."

"The name came to mind," Haggart says, "because most of the audience was composed of kids from such Chicago suburbs as Oak Park and Winnetka. It could just as easily have been *Big Noise from Oak Park*."

Haggart and Bauduc soon recorded the number and Bauduc thinks it sold 35,000 records in the Chicago area alone within a month. A number of imitators quickly tried to get the sound. "One well-known bass player thought I did it with my fingertips," says Haggart, "and he worked on it for weeks and couldn't figure it out." The Jimmy Dorsey band took a run at the number but had to use three men —neither the bass player nor the drummer could whistle properly, so trumpeter Charlie Teagarden whistled.

Soon after Bing married Kathy Grant, the Crosby clan met at his house in Holmby Hills, Los Angeles, for their mother's birthday. Standing are: *(from left)* Everett, Bing, Larry, Ted and Bob. Sisters Catherine and Mary Rose sit with their mother, who has since died, as has Everett. Larry works for Bing, and Ted is a rainmaker in Opportunity, Washington.

On Ulithi *(below)* and other embattled South Pacific atolls, Lieutenant Crosby and his "Merry Men of the Marines" won ringing applause during World War II from hot, homesick GIs whose favorite request number was *White Christmas*.

51

Do people still want to hear it? "Every single night," says Haggart. "It does get a little tiring."

Aside from diversions like *Big Noise*, the Crosby crew was serious about music. Matlock, Haggart and Rodin went to the best sources for material or inspiration: to King Oliver's Jazz Band for *Dixieland Shuffle* (alias *Riverside Blues*) and *Royal Garden Blues;* to Louis Armstrong for *Savoy Blues, Stomp Off Let's Go* and *Muskrat Ramble;* to The Original Dixieland Jazz Band for *At the Jazz Band Ball;* to Jelly Roll Morton for *Wolverine Blues;* to blues singers Big Bill Broonzy (*Louise, Louise; It Was Only a Dream*); and to Kokomo Arnold (*Milk Cow Blues*). They gave old jazz classics a new lease on life and brought authentic blues to an audience generally unfamiliar with its message.

The Bobcats, an eight-piece combo made up of the rhythm section plus the strongest sidemen, won additional popularity for the band, on records and in person, by delivering fresh and flowing Dixieland of the highest caliber. The Bobcat numbers not only made good listening but gave the musicians a chance to improvise in an unfettered small-group context after which they could tackle their parts in the sections with renewed creative vigor.

When war came and the draft began taking sidemen, the band decided to break up rather than continue with less talented substitutes. In a final July 1942 recording session they produced Crosby versions of *Anchors Aweigh, Semper Paratus,* the *Army Air Corps* song and *The Marines' Hymn.*

Bob Crosby joined the Marines in 1944, causing his brother Bing to remark: "This just changed the odds on the war and made the Japanese 8 to 5. Remind me to get rid of my war bonds."

Bob went in as an aviation specialist and was transferred immediately to the 5th Marine Division as a line officer with the rank of second lieutenant. A second lieutenant he remained at his own request until he returned to the U.S. after VJ-day. Bob was slated for combat duty, but in Hawaii the brass discovered his morale-building talents and put him in charge of a 30-man entertainment unit.

A couple of cargo planes for a song

"Members of the 120th Divisional Band were made available to me," he recalls, in a conversation with Barbara Wilkins of the Time•Life News Service, "but the only thing I'd heard them play was *The Marines' Hymn.* I started walking around the tents where some of the guys in the band were living when I saw one tent with a patch of marijuana growing beside it. I walked in and said, 'What instruments do you guys play?' That's how I got the nucleus of my first group."

The show Bob put together included a very good jazz band, a hypnotist, a comedian, and two essentials for entertaining enlisted men—a hillbilly fiddle and a guitar. Bob wanted to get the show out to combat areas but transportation was scarce. On the advice of General Holland M. ("Howlin' Mad") Smith, Bob sang a few choruses of *The Rose of Tralee* to Commanding General Pat Mulcahy of the Marine Air Wing, asked for and got two C-46 cargo planes. The group covered 29,000 miles in four months.

"We could perform as a full group," says Bob, "or we could splinter off a section that could even go entertain eight guys manning a radar station. We were always in combat areas. We'd even have a jitterbug contest with guys par-ticipating. In the forward area, of course, there were no girls."

With a second group of 60, Bob entertained at all the islands. "We went to Guam, Saipan, Green Islands, Emirau, Ulithi, everywhere," he says. "But a musician stops being a musician and becomes a stretcher bearer when there is combat. I lost some boys on Iwo Jima who were serving as stretcher bearers."

Soon after VJ-day Bob received secret orders to go to Washington, D.C. "I ran into Eddy Duchin on the plane and neither of us said a word to each other about where we were going or why. We were both under secret orders—to play a bond rally. And on the same program."

After the war Bob put together a new band, briefly, but the world had changed. Patrons preferred sweet stuff in 1946, ballads and easy tempos. "They got all the excitement they wanted during the war," Bob explained, remembering how Marines at Bougainville had asked for *White Christmas* instead of *March of the Bob Cats.* "Now they want to settle down and dance quietly." The band had little success with the new trend and broke up.

Years after the Crosby band had broken up, it was reunited, in part, for a gig at New York's Rainbow Grill. Jazz critic John Wilson thought the veterans had "weathered the years

Bob worked as a single and made a few movies, doing a particularly effective job as a Rudy Vallee crooner in *The Five Pennies*. He did well in CBS and NBC TV shows produced by Gil Rodin and frequently revived the old band or just the Bobcats for record dates or club engagements. In 1964 he put together a nine-piece group for a tour of Japan, Okinawa and the Philippines, and in 1966 New York's Rainbow Grill jumped for six weeks to the sounds of Bob Crosby's Bobcats, featuring Yank Lawson, Matty Matlock, Eddie Miller and Bob Haggart. Leopold Stokowski congratulated them after one performance of *South Rampart Street Parade* for getting such sounds with so few players "without being imprisoned by the usual bars and notes that limit other professionals."

Today Crosby, who describes himself as "the only guy in the band business who made it without talent," lives in La Jolla, California, with his second wife, June. They have five children. Cathy, the eldest, had a brief acting career and then married a Texas oil man. Christopher appeared with his father at the Rainbow Grill in New York's Rockefeller Center and has been singing with some success.

Gil Rodin, who studied television on the GI Bill, is both a TV and record producer and a vice president of Kapp Records and MCA Music. Yank Lawson and Bob Haggart are co-leaders of The World's Greatest Jazz Band, which includes Billy Butterfield among other stars.

Matty Matlock is an arranger on the West coast. Ray Bauduc, whose wife Edna inherited a fortune, lives in comfortable retirement in Texas. Nappy Lamare is playing and teaching in Los Angeles. Eddie Miller is back in New Orleans, a permanent member of Pete Fountain's successful small band which is not too unlike the Bobcats. Jess Stacy is retired but still plays for an occasional wedding or bar mitzvah.

Though it seems doubtful that the original Crosby band will ever ride again, the band's work remains its monument. It was summed up by Duke Ellington in these words: "A band with an amazing amount of color. We feel that here the tan has attained a very luxurious lustre, perhaps through absorption. However that may be, a truly gutbucket band, capable of really getting down there."

—DAN MORGENSTERN

well" and said they drove into *Big Noise from Winnetka* and their other classics "with the high-spirited attack that was a Bobcat hallmark." Yank Lawson (trumpet), Matty Matlock (clarinet) and Bob Haggart (bass) were ably seconded by such sterling replacements as Cutty Cutshall (trombone), Cliff Leeman (drums) and Bob Wilber (soprano sax).

The Music in This Volume

Few numbers so quickly bring a pleased, remembering smile to the faces of old swing fans as *A String of Pearls*. It is unmistakable Miller—the stylish sound, the light but strong beat, the confident ensemble work and that golden trumpet solo. The commanding introduction, with the same note sounding four times, an octave lower each time, ushers in the melody, played in harmony by three saxes. A wailing alto sax takes the tune, then turns it over to the full-voiced tenor, and over the ascending sax figures comes the trumpet.

Jerry Gray remembers how he wrote *A String of Pearls*. "I was young and still single and living at home in Somerville, outside Boston. My folks were at the movies and I sat down at the piano in the dark and it came to me, the whole thing—the introduction, the melody and the arrangement, and by the time the folks came back I had the whole thing in my head. It was that simple, just took me a couple of hours. Then Glenn got it and changed it a little bit here and there and we added Bobby Hackett's trumpet which really helped it a lot. The thing became an instant success so Glenn put me on composing instead of just arranging. *A String of Pearls*, I guess, was the fastest work I ever did—the fastest and the biggest."

This song would never have gone anywhere in its original form. Sam Stept first wrote the tune for a lyric entitled *Anywhere the Bluebird Goes*, but Charles Tobias and Lew Brown put new words to it, and when America went to war *Don't Sit under the Apple Tree* was suddenly a very timely piece to play and sing. Glenn Miller gave it a no-nonsense arrangement, starting out fast and bouncy, letting muted trumpets have their chance before turning the rest of the number over to Tex Beneke (who sings it again in this recording) and the other vocalists. Metronome's critics gave the number a glum B-minus but the public marked it higher. In mid-1942, as the boys were marching, sailing and flying off to battle, *Don't Sit under the Apple Tree* was fourth on Down Beat's list of most-played records.

The sensual tone, the soaring phrases, the soft embellishments all mark *Warm Valley* with the style of Johnny Hodges. Everything in this lovely Ellington work plays up to the alto saxophone—the close-harmony brass and the respectful trumpet are careful not to break the mood that the sax sets from the wistful beginning to the questioning end. Hodges played for Ellington for 38 years. He started out on the soprano sax—an instrument most jazz men looked on as a joke except when Johnny or Sidney Bechet played it—but he soon switched to the alto. "Most earlier players," writes Barry Ulanov, "had merely doodled with the instrument, but Hodges in 1928 already possessed a fully developed mature style distinguished by a warm broad tone, inflections intensely hot but never coarse and a powerful beat. He seems to have an inexhaustible supply of ravishing melodic phrases in all moods and tempos." A thoughtful musician, Hodges constantly worked over his musical ideas and challenged the resources of his instrument with long leaps and agile runs—like those heard in *Warm Valley*. "He's the only man I know who can pick up a cold horn and play it without tuning up," said Duke Ellington.

Hodges was 63 and still playing beautifully when he died in May 1970. Skeets Herfurt, who knows every record Hodges ever made, played Johnny's alto part for this album only a few days after his mentor died. "I felt very choky about it," Skeets says, "I've learned more and gained more from Johnny than from any other musician I know. Playing *Warm Valley* was very nostalgic and very sad." It was a nostalgic occasion too for the others playing with him and when Skeets finished the number they all broke into prolonged applause.

A century ago the bishop of Calcutta, on returning home from a missionary trip to Africa, related that in the region near Victoria Falls he had heard a native song strikingly like *Swing Low, Sweet Chariot*. He learned from the natives that it was inspired by the legend of a dying chief who was put in his canoe, as was the tribal custom, and pushed down the Zambezi River toward the great falls. Just as the canoe reached the brink, a chariot descended through the mists and carried the chief to the heavens. An American legend gives the song another origin: A slave in Tennessee, sold and about to be separated from her daughter, was ready to throw the child and herself into the Cumberland River when an old woman halted her, saying, "Let me read the Lord's scroll to you and let the chariot of the Lord swing low." The mother was reconciled and her story passed into song.

In actual fact, such songs as *Swing Low* may be derived from the work songs African boatmen used to sing as they paddled the rivers. But, like all spirituals, *Swing Low* is more closely related to the white man's hymns which the slaves heard and sang in church. The Fisk Jubilee Singers made the song popular on their tours a century ago and Anton Dvořák, in the first movement of his New World Symphony, gave the melody to a flute for a brief solo. (That famous *Going Home* theme in the second movement sounds like a spiritual but isn't: Dvořák wrote it himself.)

This Dorsey arrangement gives the melody to almost everybody in the band, starting with a muted trombone that sounds as light as a trumpet. The trumpet sings it, the saxes take it first soulfully, then irreverently, and eventually everybody has at it with an odd mixture of accented beats and unexpected juxtapositions of figures and harmonies. Deane Kincaide, who arranged this version, remembers that "I took a lot of stuff from some race records by Mitchell's Christian Singers and made a sort of hodgepodge of what they did and what I used to do when I was arranging for Bob Crosby."

Band 5 FLYING HOME
Lionel Hampton version

The late Malcolm X described his first encounter with *Flying Home* in his *Autobiography*. He was at the Savoy Ballroom in Harlem where Lionel Hampton was appearing. "I went a couple of rounds with the girls from the sidelines," Malcolm wrote. "People kept shouting for Hamp's *Flying Home* and

finally he did it. I had never seen such fever-heat dancing. I could believe the story I'd heard about this number—that once in the Apollo, Hamp's *Flying Home* had made some reefer-smoking Negro in the second balcony believe he could fly. So he tried and jumped—and broke his leg, an event later immortalized in song when Earl Hines wrote *Second Balcony Jump*." Hamp's famous hot number had such a wide reputation for breaking up places that once, in Connecticut, police forbade him to play it in a theater because they thought the balcony would collapse when the crowd warmed up.

All this frenzy was aroused by a man whose instrument is one of the gentlest in the band—the vibraphone, a sort of xylophone with metal resonators, each equipped with a tiny electric-powered fan which adds vibrato to that resonator's note. Hamp was a drummer who came upon the vibraphone when Louis Armstrong took him along on a recording date. Hamp was playing it in small bands around Los Angeles when Benny Goodman heard and hired him. With Hamp, the Goodman trio —Gene Krupa, Teddy Wilson and Benny—became a quartet. While he was with Benny, Hamp remembers, "We were flying back to Atlantic City. It was my first plane ride and I was humming a riff to myself. Somebody asked me what I was doing and I said I was just amusing myself. What I was really doing was taking my mind off the plane ride." In Atlantic City, the quartet worked the riff up into a number and there was, of course, only one name for it.

On the bandstand, *Flying Home* runs for six minutes or nine or, when both the crowd and band are going nonstop, for as long as 20 minutes. The recorded version runs about three. A phrase on the vibes gets the band going in medium up-tempo. It comes back to ride over a set of gutty saxophone riffs. Then the tenor sax slips in with an "Ah, So Fair" lick from *Martha*. It stays around for a long set of variations, then heats things up by sticking to a single note while the trombones rasp beneath. The heat rises when the vibes push the trumpet up higher and higher, and with ra-ta-ta-ta-ta-ta-ta BAM! the band riffs out. Hamp, as fine a band leader as he is a vibes soloist, is still playing tirelessly. A few years ago, dubbed "The Vibes President of the United States," he was given New York's highest cultural honor, the Handel Medallion, named after old George Frideric who could swing a mean concerto grosso in his day.

Band 1 JERSEY BOUNCE
Benny Goodman version

It was a Swing Era rule that if one band made a big hit with a song no other band would get very far with it. *Jersey Bounce* broke the rule. Benny Goodman and Glenn Miller both made best sellers of it. The jumpy little tune was created by a saxophonist named Bobby Plater. Mel Powell arranged it for Goodman. A gifted pianist, Powell gave himself a catchy introduction, a succession of breaks rippling through the piece and some modern harmonies in his solo near the end. He also found ways to give the tenor sax a ripe solo, the boss some high clarinet and the trombone a little raw work.

Powell was an early intellectual of the Swing Era. As a precocious New York schoolboy, he kept trying out his own compositions on his piano teacher who, he recalls, "seemed to prefer Mozart." Powell turned to jazz full time at 14, after graduating from high school. He auditioned for Goodman when he was only 18 and was, as Goodman remembers it, "so scared that I had to ask my secretary to help me decide whether he was any good—I couldn't tell." Powell became soloist and arranger for Goodman and later for Glenn Miller's Army Air Force Band. After the war, finding band life too hard, he took a job as a movie studio pianist where his major assignment was playing backgrounds for cartoons. He found that even harder. The constant glissandos he had to play blistered his knuckles as he ran them up and down the keyboard until one day a fellow worker, Andre Previn, showed him an easier way: play them with a comb.

Turning more and more to serious music, Powell studied under Paul Hindemith, became an admired and influential composer of electronic music and wound up as chairman of the Composition Faculty at the Yale Music School and, now, as Dean of Music at the California Institute of Art—a long bounce from Jersey.

Band 2 I CRIED FOR YOU
Harry James version

This was one of the first numbers Helen Forrest recorded with Harry James. Harry Rodgers, the arranger who also played trombone for James, remembers how Helen met Harry. "She was singing with Goodman," he says "and wanted to try something of her own, so she came over to the studio to ask me to make a couple of arrangements for her. Harry came in and I went over to tell him what I was doing. 'That Helen Forrest?' he asked. 'I'd like to meet her.' I was surprised he didn't know her, so I introduced them and a couple of months later she left Goodman and came over."

Miss Forrest sings *I Cried for You* again for this album. At the studio, conductor Billy May went over the number. "Helen," he said, "do you know you're hitting a D-flat in the original?" She knew it, Helen replied, "although Harry wouldn't tell me what the note was. He thought if I knew how high I was going, it would frighten me." "Well," said May, "time passes and I was just wondering. . ." and he started the number. "Working in a studio where your voice doesn't really open up," says Helen, "it's hard to tell exactly what you're doing. So at the end I asked Billy how I'd done and he said, 'Don't worry, you're hitting your note.'"

Helen has retained not only her high D-flat but also the impeccable skills that made her the nonpareil among big-band singers. "She was a musician's singer," says Rodgers. "She phrased good, sang with feeling but always clear, no mumbling. I listened to her from brass sections for six years and she got better all the time." Sam Marowitz, who was Harry James's saxophonist, still speaks of Helen with affection and admiration: "You could tune your horn to her voice even at the first show in the morning at the Paramount theater. She was always right and if you weren't with her, you were wrong."

Band 3 BASIE BOOGIE
Count Basie version

"Boogie-woogie?" said a long-hair musician years ago on being introduced to this eight-to-the-bar piano style, "We've had it around for a thousand years, only we call it *ostinato*." Not quite a thousand years, actually. *Ostinato*, which is the persistent repetition throughout a composition of a single phrase, goes back to twelfth century motets and was a favorite device of renaissance and baroque music. In the 1880s or '90s, blues pianists in lumber and construction camps of the south or west used the repetitive device in a style called "fast Western." In the 1920s this was picked up by pianists around Chicago who developed it into the boogie style: a walking-bass figure kept going by the left hand while the right hand plays against it with all kinds of counterpoint, free variations and broken octave tremolos.

Boogie-woogie might never have gotten out of Chicago if John Hammond in 1935 hadn't come upon a record made by Meade Lux Lewis in 1929. Hammond found Lewis washing cars in a garage and brought him to New York where Lewis, along with Albert Ammons and Pete Johnson, made boogie-woogie popular in the 52nd Street and Village jazz joints. Count Basie's boogie is a piano piece with orchestral accompaniment. At first, the piano is more blues than boogie but soon it rolls full out with the boogie bass and gets the band rolling.

The name boogie-woogie, incidentally, was invented by Pinetop Smith, an erratic and talented pianist who adopted the expression "pitchin' boogie," which meant throwing a rent party. All that anyone really remembers of Pinetop now is one number, *Pinetop's Boogie Woogie*, which he recorded before he died in a dance-hall brawl in 1929.

Band 4 CHARLESTON ALLEY
Charlie Barnet version

Like so many other swing tunes, *Charleston Alley* was born without a name, a danceable tune written in 1940 by Horace Henderson, Fletcher's younger brother. "We didn't name things until we needed them," Charlie Barnet explains. "There was no reason for a song to have a name until it was recorded. Until then it was just a number. And a lot of titles we thought up were in jokes, or about something that happened to the boys." In this case, what had happened to Barnet's boys was a little trouble in Charleston's red-light district that landed some of them in jail for the night. "I called the tune *Charleston Alley*," says Charlie drily, "to remind them of their indiscretions."

The band introduced the number at the College Inn in Chicago's Sherman Hotel and it caught on right away. The public never got tired of it and neither did the players—they made three different recordings of it. In this 1941 version the trumpet opens with an emphatic half chorus, the tenor sax boots along over the drums, and after a set of chromatically descending chords, the soprano sax leads the sax section for a half chorus, then the trumpet blows in for an easygoing reprise. "In the idiom of swing music," says Barnet, "*Charleston Alley* was right between the eyes. Nobody had to stretch to understand it."

Band 5 AIR MAIL SPECIAL
Benny Goodman version

In a recording studio, after five or six tries at a number there was nothing the sidemen hated to hear more than the sound engineer saying, "Let's go for another" or "Let's take it again" or "We'll hold that one for a safety." What they loved to hear him say was "Good enough to keep" and when, in March 1941, the engineer applied those welcome words to a number Benny Goodman and the sextet had just finished, Benny decided to use them as the title. Benny did the number again with his big band a couple of months later at a time when his arch rival, Artie Shaw, was having great success with his *Special Delivery Stomp*. So Goodman changed *Good Enough to Keep* to *Air Mail Special* and that is its name today.

The piece is based, as so many Goodman head numbers were, on a Charlie Christian riff—the nervous insistent phrase that keeps pushing its way in all through the piece. The first solo is a classic show of single-string guitar improvising. After a clarinet chorus, and a querulous growl trumpet, comes a famous tenor-sax solo in a vigorous and earthy style. Billy Butterfield, who played trumpet for the big band version, remembers how popular *Air Mail Special* was. "The audience would break up our program and shout and holler for *Air Mail*. It was quite a barn burner."

Band 1 9:20 SPECIAL
Count Basie version

9:20 Special is vintage Basie, showing off the precision and sensitivity and carefully leashed strength of his 1941 band. Trumpets, saxes and rhythm go at it together, the muted horns with a light propulsive swing and the saxes with a feathery touch. The styles of the soloists are easy to identify. The piano notes are placed carefully and economically, the trumpet is clean and tight over the ensemble and the tenor sax is fluent and inventive. Why the title? The band had come to the recording studio after a night's work in Chicago and by the time they finished this number it was 9:20 a.m.

Band 2 THE MAN I LOVE
Benny Goodman version

Very few songs—and certainly none as great as this one—ever had as tough a time trying to break into show business as The Man I Love. George Gershwin composed it in 1923 as the verse for a song he was writing for Lady Be Good. But it was so overpowering that he threw away the chorus and just kept the verse. When Otto Kahn, the famous angel of the opera, was asked to help back Lady Be Good, he said he wasn't interested—until he was told that the score included a tune that had stuck in his mind ever since Gershwin had played it for him some months before. So, because of The Man I Love, Kahn put up $10,000 and right after the Philadelphia tryout, the producer yanked the song—it had left the audiences cold. In 1927 Gershwin tried again, using The Man I Love in his first version of Strike Up the Band. It didn't make it then either—and neither did the show. Refusing to give up, Gershwin put it into Rosalie as a number for Marilyn Miller. It came right out.

Meanwhile, the song was not languishing. Eva Gauthier, the distinguished French art-song singer, introduced it in a 1925 recital at which Gershwin was her accompanist. Lady Mountbatten, wife of the future war hero and viceroy of India, coaxed an autographed copy out of Gershwin and asked her favorite London band, the Berkeley Square Orchestra, to play it. Other bands in London took it up, then bands in Paris and finally some in the U.S. When, in 1930, Gershwin gave it a last try and put The Man I Love into his second (and successful) version of Strike Up the Band, it sounded so familiar that it had to come out.

Why, since it had made its way into the permanent popular repertory, couldn't Man I Love make it on Broadway? "It has a certain slow lilt," Gershwin himself explained, "that subtly disturbs the audience. The melody is not easy to catch—it presents too many chromatic pitfalls. Hardly anybody whistles it or hums it correctly without the support of a piano or some other instrument." Helen Forrest, who made a memorable rendition of it 30 years ago with Benny Goodman, says it more succinctly. "It's a singer's song," she remarked, when she did it again for this album.

Band 3 SUMMIT RIDGE DRIVE
Artie Shaw version

This is jaunty, small-scale Shaw—just Artie and a quintet. "But I didn't want to use that word, quintet, for the group" says Shaw, "so I called it the Gramercy Five, after the New York telephone exchange." The piece itself was named after Artie's Hollywood home address, 1426 Summit Ridge Drive, where he rehearsed the group. The number brought to jazz the unfamiliar jangle of the harpsichord, used for the first time in a swing band. "Artie phoned me," recalls pianist Johnny Guarnieri,

"and asked, 'Johnny, you know how to play the harpsichord?' 'Sure,' I said, figuring I could find out pretty easily. 'Come on over,' Artie said, 'we're cutting a side with one tomorrow.'" When he got to the Summit Drive apartment and confronted the instrument, Guarnieri had to admit that he'd never laid a finger on one before. "But Artie didn't mind. I guess he liked my nerve. I sat down at the harpsichord—I remember it was built by a guy who lived in Ypsilanti, Michigan—and I got the hang pretty fast, except I had trouble in runs where I had to use the fourth and fifth fingers. The action is different from a piano and you have to hit sharply with all the fingers or the notes won't sound. I went home and practiced until I could trill with the fourth and fifth fingers for 20 seconds. Then I was O.K."

Summit Ridge had not gotten very far when Shaw broke up his band a few months later and went into the Navy. "But when I got out in 1945," Artie says, "I found I had a hit in Summit. I think, to use a clumsy expression, it's because it was a record ahead of its time." Others thought it was because of the harpsichord—but not Metronome's reviewer. "The harpsichord is novel," he wrote sternly, "but so is ground glass in a ham sandwich."

Band 4 ADIOS
Glenn Miller version

Almost any composer would have been grateful to a band for doing as well by his music as Glenn Miller did in his ingratiating performance of Adios. But Enric Madriguera, who composed Adios and was a leading conductor of Latin music, hated swing. Madriguera, who had studied the violin under Leopold Auer, the renowned teacher of Heifetz and Elman, denounced swing as "just a little germ that spread fast. It is not the type of music for America. It is blatant and makes people neurotic. It comes from the world's distress and was born out of people trying to forget by going to nightclubs and drinking."

To this attack on his art, Glenn Miller turned the other cheek, with a beautifully conceived rendition of Madriguera's song. The melody and the counter melody flow along on reeds and brass. The trombones, with a flourish of aluminum derbies in front of the bells, achieve a special Miller sound. The trumpet sings muted solos. Adios shows how pleasingly Glenn Miller's band could pour out music like hot fudge while never losing its parade-ground precision.

Band 5 GOLDEN WEDDING
Woody Herman version

Anyone who has had to sit through the pupil recitals that piano teachers inflict on parents will recognize this little piece as something called La Cinquantaine. It means Golden Wedding, of course, and is the only claim to musical immortality left by the late Gabriel-Marie, a French composer who conducted provincial symphony orchestras in France around the turn of the century. He wrote Cinquantaine in 1887, referring to it as "a tune in the antique style" and arranging it first for violin or cello, later for the piano. Jiggs Noble arranged the Woody Herman version largely for the drums. At the start the tom-toms beat behind the Arabic wail of the clarinet. After some general whomping and wailing, with the trumpet sputtering around, the drummer gets different pitches out of two tom-toms before working himself into a fury on the snares and cymbals. Then he settles back to take on the rest of the band and at the end drives the clarinet clear out of its highest A above high C.

Band 1 BEYOND THE BLUE HORIZON
Artie Shaw version

Jeanette MacDonald introduced *Beyond the Blue Horizon* in a 1930 film called *Monte Carlo*. She sang it sitting in a train compartment en route to the Riviera and, as she passed through the countryside, peasants in the fields sang back at her in harmony. The movie arrangement, full of clickety-clacking rails and locomotive whoo-whoos, was, composer Leo Robins boasted, "the talk of the movie industry at the time." (Jeanette revived the song in 1944's *Follow the Boys*.) Artie Shaw got along fine without iron-horse effects: his version is full of the reasons his music was almost never boring—a skillful use of strings, a variety of textures, a constant moving from strings to reeds to brass and back to strings, the injection of a jazz chorus into a somewhat sweet mixture. The opening, dreamy and slow, is a fooler. The ensemble picks up the pace, bending the notes slightly. The firm-toned clarinet comes on and the trombone butts in, playing jazz jokes over the strings. The original trombonist was Ray Coniff and his playing gave no hint of what he does today with his full-blown Ray Coniff singers. *Metronome* in 1940 gave *Horizon* an "A—best Shaw side to date."

Band 2 CHATTANOOGA CHOO CHOO
Glenn Miller version

"I guess I have maybe a dozen keys to Chattanooga," remarks Tex Beneke, who sang *Chattanooga Choo Choo* in both the original recording and in this one. "The folks there always treat me well." This Glenn Miller landmark, written in 1941 by Mack Gordon and Harry Warren, was introduced by Miller in the movie *Sun Valley Serenade* and has been played in several films since. The Andrews Sisters latched on to it and sold 250,000 records. Miller sold more than a million.

The train introduction carries over into the first chorus with the saxes and brasses riding along fast. Then they keep the wheels moving in 6/8 time while Beneke goes into the give-and-take that he, the Four Modernaires and Marion Hutton made memorable. "When we played *Choo Choo* in *Sun Valley Serenade*," says Beneke, "we musicians didn't care much for it. But Glenn knew what appealed to an audience—he was seldom wrong on that. Today everywhere I go I have to play *Choo Choo* two or three times an evening. To do a tune over and over again for 30 years would drive a man crazy except for that saving feeling of appreciation from the audience. The reaction is always good and makes me feel good too."

Band 3 AUTUMN NOCTURNE
Claude Thornhill version

Claude Thornhill felt most at home in the quieter sectors of swing, setting off his own tasteful piano playing with soft, sophisticated arrangements that always deferred to the melody. *Autumn Nocturne*, a sad-sweet little piece, was arranged by Thornhill and, next to his memorable *Snowfall*, was his biggest request number. This is the way it was done by his first band in 1941. The piano introduces the theme, playing it prettily over a soft, ensemble counter melody. The band swells the tune and the piano resumes. Next comes a lovely, limpid chorus originally played by Irving Fazola, one of the last of the great New Orleans clarinetists. And then it is the piano again winding up what is, in effect, a small, piano tone poem.

Band 4 BENNY RIDES AGAIN
Benny Goodman version

Benny Goodman's is the only bad back that has ever been celebrated musically. *Slipped Disc* commemorates his spinal troubles and *Benny Rides Again* hails his return to the band in 1941 after a three-month siege. For the occasion, Eddie Sauter wrote and arranged one of the most advanced swing numbers of the time. Compared to its changing textures, its minor-key brass ensembles and its complex harmonies, such famous Goodman numbers as *Blue Skies* or *Stomping at the Savoy* seem Early American Swing. Clipped phrases, a growling trumpet, gutty saxes and brasses decorate the opening segment. The tom-toms sound and the clarinet rides in for a long ensemble under the saxes and then sets out on a series of brilliant solos—piercing, plaintive, commanding.

"With Benny out sick," says Sauter, one of the most admired and adventurous popular-music arrangers then and now, "I had time to fool around. I'd never had the courage to do this type of thing before. Benny always thought my arrangements were too classical. In *Benny Rides Again*, there's some *Caucasian Sketches*, *Sing, Sing, Sing*, a little country Brahms, very bad Vaughn-Williams, a little *Clarinet à la King*—they're all involved in it."

The original recording ran four minutes, 40 seconds, too long for the standard ten-inch record, so it appeared as Goodman's first twelve-incher with Helen Forrest singing *The Man I Love* on the other side.

Band 1 THE MOLE
Harry James version

LeRoy Holmes, Harry James's arranger, had stayed up all night doing a special rush order. James needed a jumpy piece for the B side of a record and Holmes had set down an intriguing rhythmic phrase with a simple melody on top. "It's fine," said Harry when Holmes handed it to him. "What do you want to call it?" "I don't know," Holmes replied. "I'm tired and I'm going to bed." After the recording James asked the band for ideas for a title. One sideman said that the repeated figure reminded him of an underground character called the Mole who was the current villain of the Dick Tracy comic strip. The title has always annoyed Holmes—he had hoped for something exotic. *The Mole* became one of Harry's bigger hits.

The title character, played on the baritone sax, keeps running in and out of the piece, scurrying into the introduction, getting underfoot through the easy muted brass, moving with the strings, and is still stumbling around when, after a fat tenor sax bit, everything ends on an up-the-scale flare.

Somewhere in the number there is a mistake: that's the way James himself always wanted it. Harry was superstitious—he came of a circus family—and in one of his early recordings, he worried about a mistake he had let get by. When the piece became one of Harry's first hits, he decided that was an omen. From then on, if a recording sounded too good to him, he'd say uneasily: "Let's do it again." He wasn't satisfied until the piece was a little flawed—nothing anyone else would notice, but just short of perfection.

reflects the man. Woody is not a worrier. When he set up his second band (the first of his Herds) he told the players, most of them new to him, that he'd thrown away his arrangements but they'd get along. That was all right for most of the standards, which the men had played elsewhere, but none of them had ever touched *Blue Flame* which was all Woody's. So Woody sang them a chorus and told them to take it any way they felt like. By the time Woody did get an arrangement, the men had worked out their own *Blue Flame* and didn't need it.

Band 2 **A SMO-O-O-TH ONE**
Benny Goodman version

Benny was a little late for a studio date in 1941 and, while hanging around, the other members of his sextet put on a small jam session to warm themselves up and help the engineers adjust their equipment. They took their cues from Charlie Christian as he kept trying out riffs on his electric guitar. He found one they all liked and they went to town with it. Usually, such impromptu numbers were played and forgotten, but this one, by chance recorded on the spot, was many years later issued as *Waiting for Benny*. You'll easily identify in *A Smo-o-o-th One*, one of Benny's best-known sextet numbers, the riff that the band liked and recorded that same day. It is a quirky phrase introduced by trumpet, tenor sax and guitar. It moves over the clarinet, romps past a growl trumpet and a booting tenor sax, answers the repeated "smack" on the trumpet and leads into the guitar solo near the end.

After hearing Christian play a session with Goodman, Eddie Durham, the first jazzman to use an electric guitar, remembers the days back in Oklahoma when Charlie was switching from the piano. "I never saw a guy learn to play faster than him," he said, "and I'll never forget that beat-up five-dollar wooden guitar he used to take to jam sessions."

In this number, as in *Air Mail Special*, the guitar's rhythm pulls the group along while the guitarist himself breaks away into offbeat accents and surprising patterns. The effect of Christian's inventiveness and harmonic daring spread beyond Goodman's band. Charlie was the first important influence on such future jazz radicals as Charlie Parker, Dizzy Gillespie and Thelonius Monk, with whom he used to play in after-work sessions in Harlem before his death of tuberculosis at the age of 22.

Band 3 **BLUE FLAME**
Woody Herman version

Everybody in the swing years knew that the sound of *Woodchopper's Ball* meant Woody Herman coming on; the strains of *Blue Flame* meant Woody and his clarinet were signing off. This theme song is the bluest of the blues that were the specialty of Herman's first great band—THE BAND THAT PLAYS THE BLUES. It was written by Jiggs Noble, Herman's arranger, and Joe Bishop, his part-time flugelhorn player. The blue mood is set right off by low trombones and saxes with the clarinet filling in. Then the trombone comes on in the "dirty" (rough, growling) style for which Neil Reed, Herman's star trombonist, was noted. The clarinet joins in, slipping in and out until the final stretch and the sustained chord on which the music falls away.

The piece is in Herman's most relaxed style, one that

Band 4 **WELL, GIT IT!**
Tommy Dorsey version

"Well, Git It!" says Sy Oliver, its composer, "started out to be *Bugle Blues*, but when I got through there was nothing in it that could be identified as a bugle, so I changed the name and opening lines." The piece is basically a 16-bar blues. It opens with a now-famous two-trumpet display, played originally by Ziggy Elman and Chuck Peterson. A trombone takes over on a one-note figure and wild modulation builds to solos by a loose clarinet and a stiff tenor sax. The piano runs in and then a trumpet climbs up the chromatics to a high-pitched dialogue with another trumpeter.

One of the most powerful of swing's brass blowers, Elman began music as a five-year-old by studying the violin "because my father enjoyed it." As he grew up, Ziggy found he could play almost any instrument he tried—piano, organ, clarinet. He broke in professionally as a trombonist, took up the trumpet because it gave him chances for solo work. He was playing trumpet in a house band in Atlantic City in 1936 when Benny Goodman nabbed him. Instead of letting him sit back in the trumpet section and break in gradually, Benny handed Ziggy the first trumpet book and told him to get out there and play. Ziggy joined Tommy Dorsey in 1940 in time to contribute to *Well, Git It!* and a score of other popular Dorsey recordings.

Band 5 **PERDIDO**
Duke Ellington version

Though Juan Tizol, the Duke's valve trombonist, wrote and arranged it, *Perdido* wasn't his particular dish. His métier was the smooth, lush tone that he exploited so well in some of his other compositions like *Caravan* and *Azure*. *Perdido* is for hot horns. "We were traveling," Tizol recalls, "and I was sitting in a railroad coach tapping the window and the melody came to me. I thought, that's pretty good and I better write it down before I forget it. I gave it to the Duke that evening and he liked it." Ellington at the time was feeling a little pressed by the popularity of Count Basie and Jimmie Lunceford and wanted to challenge those free-swingers on their own ground. *Perdido* was a happy answer. A perennial Ellington favorite, it has become a staple of jam sessions.

The Ellington beat is always clear and comes on strong with the heavy, syncopated left-hand piano chords—and from then on the beat is everybody's business, not just the rhythm section's but the saxes and the trumpets too. A stentorian baritone sax takes the first chorus. Then the trumpet and tenor soloists take over—by turns sentimental, brassy, biting—and after a muttering drum and a hesitant piano, the ensemble blares a finale.

Band 1 SONG OF THE VOLGA BOATMEN
Glenn Miller version

The Song of the Volga Boatmen first became familiar to Americans through the concerts and records of Feodor Chaliapin, the legendary Russian basso who had once worked as a stevedore on the Volga and had heard the boatmen, chanting *"Ei Ukhniem, Ei Ukhneim"* (which doesn't mean anything; they're more groans than words).

As a World War II ally, Russia was newly popular with Americans in 1942 when Glenn Miller set Bill Finegan to working out this arrangement. Finegan poured in almost everything but the Volga itself. Along with the spooky bass introduction comes a whooshing that might be the wind over the steppes. Trombones play the melody in a minor key as a muted trumpet mutters in the background. The band swings heavily into the major, the alto sax offers an imaginative little solo, and then comes the most ingenious part of the piece: a brass canon, a kind of round in which the theme is tossed back and forth between trumpets and trombones while hand-claps and cymbals keep the beat. Swing critics at the time liked the rich orchestration, but it isn't certain that Chaliapin would have. "The boatmen's song," he used to complain, "is tortured for American ears."

Band 2 CONTRASTS
Jimmy Dorsey version

For a song that became an anthem of the Swing Era—heard on hundreds of stages and bandstands, on movie sets and war programs, on uncounted coast-to-coast broadcasts—*Contrasts* had an inconsequential beginning. Jimmy Dorsey wrote it when he was a kid in Shenandoah, Pennsylvania, as one of those show-off solos every young saxophonist cuts his teeth on. He called it *Oodles of Noodles* and once recorded it under that name. After he broke with his brother Tommy, he chose it as the theme song for his own band. From the first melting solo to the wistful signing off, the number is almost all in the style that was uniquely Jimmy's; the tone is full and virile, especially in the lower and middle registers, and the improvisations never slight the melody. The title itself reflects the distinctive approach of Jimmy's band in both the contrasting ensemble work and in the sudden tempo changes—from slow to fast and abruptly back again.

Band 3 STRICTLY INSTRUMENTAL
Harry James version

In 1942 Harry James felt his band was going too heavy on vocals and looked for some numbers that didn't require singers. *Strictly Instrumental* was just what he was looking for. Usually instrumentals were showcases for the band's get-off men and ensemble virtuosity, the killer-dillers that pulled the audiences away from dancing to crowd around the bandstand. This one is a quieter kind, strictly for dancing. For most of the first chorus, the muted trumpet talks back and forth with the band. The tenor sax goes at it lightheartedly. Then the trumpet is back, dancing over the counter figures and then winding up its conversation *sotto voce* with the rest of the band. The trumpet was Harry James, as it almost always was. But having a star like Harry presented a problem to the band on the rare occasions when he didn't show up. When that happened, Claude Bowen took Harry's intimate solos, Al Cuozzo played the lead parts and Nick Buono came on for those long high notes. It was probably the only time in swing history when it took a trio to blow one man's horn.

Band 4 DANCING IN THE DARK
Artie Shaw version

Arthur Schwartz and Howard Dietz were going over their score for *The Band Wagon* in 1931 at Dietz's house in Greenwich Village. What the show needed, Dietz kept saying, was a serious song, something with a philosophic message. Browsing through his bookshelf, he pulled out a volume called *Dancers in the Dark,* and quoted a few sentences from it.

Getting back home long after midnight, Schwartz sat down at his piano and in hardly more time than it took to play his idea through, composed his somber *Dancing in the Dark.* Deitz set appropriately somber words to it—"We're waltzing in the wonder of why we're here, Time hurries by—we're here and gone. . ." But the song was inordinately long and they both felt it was not what the show needed—a tune the audience would be humming on the way out of the theater. So they imported a number called *High and Low* that they had written for a London show, and *The Band Wagon* audience did go out humming its catchy phrases. But the song that is still hummed, sung, played and heard everywhere today is, of course, *Dancing in the Dark.*

In Shaw's version, the strings are always present. "Artie was excited by strings," says pianist Johnny Guarnieri. "Other bands had used them but what Artie wanted—and Artie always knew what he wanted—was a flowing effect and he kept the men working over different voicings until he got it." Strings underlie the opening brass statement, take the first chorus, comment gently on Artie's clarinet and keep flowing as Artie told them to. "Shaw's big band," said *Metronome* approvingly in 1941, "sounds as a big band should."

Band 5 AMERICAN PATROL
Glenn Miller version

John Philip Sousa didn't write all those marches he played, although it sometimes seems that way. *American Patrol* was composed by F. W. Meacham, a busy arranger of other men's music. He wrote the march in 1885 and then passed without further notice into musical history. Sousa appreciated its snappy, no-fooling phrases and used to play it early in his programs to rouse his audiences. He leaned heavily, of course, on his brasses. Jerry Gray, in arranging *Patrol* for Glenn Miller, reversed the martial order by putting the saxophones up front. Led by the baritone, they march off, the muted trumpets trotting after. A roll of drums signals a change as the band breaks into *Columbia the Gem of the Ocean* and *The Girl I Left Behind Me.*

Such interpolations are in the best military band tradition. In his first recording of *American Patrol,* done in 1909, Sousa pulled in *Hail Columbia, Dixie* and *Yankee Doodle.*

It is interesting to see what happens to military 4/4 time when a swing band takes over. Sousa, with 4/4, gets you up on your feet and marching. Glenn Miller, with 4/4 plus a little syncopation, gets you up on your feet and dancing. Of course, the old New Orleans street-marching bands knew that trick, way back at the very beginnings of jazz.

—JOSEPH KASTNER

The Musicians Who Made the Recordings in This Volume

A STRING OF PEARLS
LEADER: Glen Gray TRUMPETS: Conrad Gozzo, Shorty Sherock, Pete Candoli, Manny Klein TROMBONES: Si Zentner, Murray McEachern, Joe Howard, Benny Benson SAXOPHONES: Skeets Herfurt, Gus Bivona, Babe Russin, Chuck Gentry, Julie Jacob PIANO: Ray Sherman GUITAR: Jack Marshall BASS: Mike Rubin DRUMS: Nick Fatool SOLOS: Skeets Herfurt (alto saxophone), Babe Russin (tenor saxophone), Manny Klein (trumpet), Ray Sherman (piano)

DON'T SIT UNDER THE APPLE TREE
LEADER: Billy May TRUMPETS: Shorty Sherock, Uan Rasey, John Best, Frank Beach, John Audino TROMBONES: Milt Bernhart, Lew McCreary, Lloyd Ulyate, Dick Noel SAXOPHONES: Skeets Herfurt, Willie Schwartz, Justin Gordon, Plas Johnson, Abe Most PIANO: Ray Sherman GUITAR: Jack Marshall BASS: Rolly Bundock DRUMS: Nick Fatool VOCAL: Tex Beneke, Eileen Wilson and vocal group

WARM VALLEY
LEADER: Billy May TRUMPETS: Pete Candoli, Shorty Sherock, Frank Beach, John Audino, Uan Rasey TROMBONES: Joe Howard, Dick Nash, Lew McCreary, Lloyd Ulyate SAXOPHONES: Skeets Herfurt, Abe Most, Plas Johnson, Justin Gordon, Jack Nimitz PIANO: Ray Sherman GUITAR: Jack Marshall BASS: Rolly Bundock DRUMS: Nick Fatool SOLOS: Skeets Herfurt (alto saxophone), Shorty Sherock (trumpet)

SWING LOW, SWEET CHARIOT
LEADER: Billy May TRUMPETS: Pete Candoli, Shorty Sherock, Uan Rasey, Frank Beach, John Audino TROMBONES: Joe Howard, Milt Bernhart, Lew McCreary, Dick Nash SAXOPHONES: Skeets Herfurt, Abe Most, Justin Gordon, Plas Johnson, Chuck Gentry, Willie Schwartz PIANO: Ray Sherman GUITAR: Jack Marshall BASS: Rolly Bundock DRUMS: Nick Fatool SOLOS: Joe Howard (trombone), Pete Candoli (trumpet), Abe Most (alto saxophone), Justin Gordon (tenor saxophone)

FLYING HOME
Same as A STRING OF PEARLS with Emil Richards on vibraphone SOLOS: Emil Richards (vibes), Plas Johnson (tenor saxophone), Pete Candoli (trumpet)

JERSEY BOUNCE
LEADER: Billy May TRUMPETS: Shorty Sherock, Uan Rasey, John Best, Frank Beach TROMBONES: Dick Nash, Milt Bernhart, Lew McCreary SAXOPHONES: Skeets Herfurt, Justin Gordon, Plas Johnson, Willie Schwartz, Jack Nimitz, Abe Most PIANO: Ray Sherman GUITAR: Jack Marshall BASS: Rolly Bundock DRUMS: Nick Fatool SOLOS: Justin Gordon (tenor saxophone), Dick Nash (trombone), Abe Most (clarinet)

I CRIED FOR YOU
LEADER: Billy May TRUMPETS: Shorty Sherock, Frank Beach, John Best, Uan Rasey, Joe Graves TROMBONES: Dick Nash, Lew McCreary, Milt Bernhardt, Joe Howard SAXOPHONES: Willie Schwartz, Abe Most, Plas Johnson, Chuck Gentry VIOLINS: Lou Raderman, Jimmy Getzoff, Mischa Russel, John De Voogdt, Bob Barene, Eddie Bergman, Lenny Atkins, Isadore Roman, Irv Geller, Darrel Terwilliger VIOLAS: Sam Boghossian, Lou Kievman, Jan Hlinka CELLOS: Armand Kaproff, Kurt Reher, Nino Rosso PIANO: Ray Sherman GUITAR: Jack Marshall BASS: Rolly Bundock DRUMS: Nick Fatool VOCAL: Helen Forrest SOLO: Joe Graves (trumpet)

ORCHESTRA MANAGER: Abe Siegel
MIXER: Rex Updegraft

BASIE BOOGIE
Same as WARM VALLEY SOLOS: Pete Candoli (trumpet), Plas Johnson (tenor saxophone)

CHARLESTON ALLEY
Same as SWING LOW, SWEET CHARIOT SOLOS: Pete Candoli (trumpet), Plas Johnson (tenor saxophone)

AIR MAIL SPECIAL
LEADER: Billy May TRUMPET: Shorty Sherock CLARINET: Abe Most SAXOPHONE: Justin Gordon PIANO: Ray Sherman GUITAR: Al Hendrickson BASS: Rolly Bundock DRUMS: Nick Fatool SOLOS: Al Hendrickson (guitar), Abe Most (clarinet), Shorty Sherock (trumpet), Justin Gordon (tenor saxophone)

9:20 SPECIAL
Same as WARM VALLEY SOLOS: Skeets Herfurt (alto saxophone), Pete Candoli (trumpet), Plas Johnson (tenor saxophone), Ray Sherman (piano)

THE MAN I LOVE
LEADER: Billy May TRUMPETS: Shorty Sherock, Uan Rasey, John Audino, Frank Beach, John Best TROMBONES: Joe Howard, Milt Bernhart, Dick Nash, Lew McCreary SAXOPHONES: Willie Schwartz, Abe Most, Justin Gordon, Bill Green, Chuck Gentry PIANO: Ray Sherman GUITAR: Jack Marshall BASS: Rolly Bundock DRUMS: Nick Fatool VOCAL: Helen Forrest SOLOS: Abe Most (clarinet), John Best (trumpet)

SUMMIT RIDGE DRIVE
LEADER: Billy May TRUMPETS: Shorty Sherock CLARINET: Abe Most HARPSICHORD: Ray Sherman GUITAR: Al Hendrickson BASS: Rolly Bundock DRUMS: Nick Fatool SOLOS: Ray Sherman (harpsichord), Rolly Bundock (bass), Shorty Sherock (trumpet), Abe Most (clarinet)

ADIOS
LEADER: Billy May TRUMPETS: Pete Candoli, Shorty Sherock, Uan Rasey, Frank Beach TROMBONES: Joe Howard, Dick Nash, Lew McCreary, Lloyd Ulyate SAXOPHONES: Wilbur Schwartz, Abe Most, Justin Gordon, Plas Johnson, Chuck Gentry PIANO: Ray Sherman GUITAR: Jack Marshall BASS: Rolly Bundock DRUMS: Nick Fatool SOLOS: Shorty Sherock (muted trumpet), Joe Howard (trombone)

GOLDEN WEDDING
Same as JERSEY BOUNCE SOLOS: Shorty Sherock (trumpet), Abe Most (clarinet)

BEYOND THE BLUE HORIZON
LEADER: Billy May TRUMPETS: Shorty Sherock, Uan Rasey TROMBONE: Dick Nash SAXOPHONES: Willie Schwartz, Justin Gordon, Abe Most VIOLINS: Lou Raderman, Jimmy Getzoff, Mischa Russel, John De Voogdt, Bob Barene, Eddie Bergman, Lenny Atkins, Isadore Roman, Irv Geller, Darrel Terwilliger VIOLAS: Sam Boghossian, Lou Kievman, Jan Hlinka CELLOS: Armand Kaproff, Kurt Reher, Nino Rosso PIANO: Ray Sherman GUITAR: Jack Marshall BASS: Rolly Bundock DRUMS: Nick Fatool SOLOS: Abe Most (clarinet), Dick Nash (trombone), Jack Marshall (guitar)

CHATTANOOGA CHOO CHOO
Same as DON'T SIT UNDER THE APPLE TREE without Eileen Wilson

AUTUMN NOCTURNE
Same as SWING LOW, SWEET CHARIOT SOLOS: Ray Sherman (piano), Abe Most (clarinet)

BENNY RIDES AGAIN
Same as JERSEY BOUNCE SOLOS: Shorty Sherock (trumpet), Abe Most (clarinet)

THE MOLE
Same as I CRIED FOR YOU without vocal and with Justin Gordon added on saxophone SOLO: Justin Gordon (tenor saxophone)

A SMO-O-O-TH ONE
Same as AIR MAIL SPECIAL SOLOS: Shorty Sherock (trumpet), Justin Gordon (tenor saxphone), Abe Most (clarinet)

BLUE FLAME
LEADER: Glen Gray TRUMPETS: Conrad Gozzo, Shorty Sherock, Joe Graves, Uan Rasey TROMBONES: Joe Howard, Ed Kusby, Milt Bernhart, Lew McCreary SAXOPHONES: Skeets Herfurt, Abe Most, Babe Russin, Plas Johnson, Chuck Gentry PIANO: Ray Sherman GUITAR: Jack Marshall BASS: Mike Rubin DRUMS: Nick Fatool SOLOS: Abe Most (clarinet), Milt Bernhart (trombone), Jack Marshall (guitar)

WELL, GIT IT!
LEADER: Glen Gray TRUMPETS: Conrad Gozzo, Manny Klein, Joe Graves, Shorty Sherock, Uan Rasey TROMBONES: Joe Howard, Milt Bernhart, Lew McCreary, Si Zentner SAXOPHONES: Abe Most, Skeets Herfurt, Plas Johnson, Babe Russin, Chuck Gentry PIANO: Ray Sherman GUITAR: Jack Marshall BASS: Mike Rubin DRUMS: Irv Cottler SOLOS: Joe Graves, Shorty Sherock (trumpets), Joe Howard (trombone), Ray Sherman (piano), Abe Most (clarinet), Babe Russin (tenor saxophone)

PERDIDO
Same as WARM VALLEY SOLOS: Pete Candoli (1st solo trumpet), Shorty Sherock (2nd solo trumpet), Plas Johnson (tenor saxophone), Pete Candoli (last solo trumpet)

SONG OF THE VOLGA BOATMEN
Same as SWING LOW, SWEET CHARIOT SOLOS: Skeets Herfurt (alto saxophone), Shorty Sherock (trumpet)

CONTRASTS
Same as A STRING OF PEARLS SOLO: Skeets Herfurt (alto saxophone)

STRICTLY INSTRUMENTAL
Same as JERSEY BOUNCE SOLOS: Shorty Sherock (trumpet), Justin Gordon (tenor saxophone)

DANCING IN THE DARK
LEADER: Billy May TRUMPETS: Shorty Sherock, Uan Rasey, Frank Beach, Joe Graves TROMBONES: Lew McCreary, Joe Howard SAXOPHONES: Willie Schwartz, Abe Most, Plas Johnson, Chuck Gentry VIOLINS: Lon Raderman, Jimmy Getzoff, Mischa Russel, John De Voogdt, Bob Barene, Eddie Bergman, Lenny Atkins, Isadore Roman, Irv Geller, Darrel Terwilliger VIOLAS: Sam Boghossian, Lou Kievman, Jan Hlinka CELLOS: Armand Kaproff, Kurt Reher, Nino Rosso PIANO: Ray Sherman GUITAR: Jack Marshall BASS: Rolly Bundock DRUMS: Nick Fatool SOLOS: Abe Most (clarinet), Joe Graves (trumpet)

AMERICAN PATROL
LEADER: Billy May TRUMPETS: Shorty Sherock, Frank Beach, John Best, Uan Rasey, John Audino TROMBONES: Milt Bernhart, Dick Nash, Joe Howard, Lew McCreary SAXOPHONES: Willie Schwartz, Abe Most, Justin Gordon, Bill Green, Chuck Gentry PIANO: Ray Sherman GUITAR: Jack Marshall BASS: Rolly Bundock DRUMS: Nick Fatool SOLO: Shorty Sherock (trumpet)

Discography

The original recordings of the
selections re-created in this volume

A STRING OF PEARLS
Composer and arranger: Jerry Gray.
Recorded for Bluebird November 3, 1941

TRUMPETS	SAXOPHONES
Mickey McMickle	°Babe Russin
°John Best	°Tex Beneke
°Billy May	°Willie Schwartz
Alec Fila	Ernie Caceres
TROMBONES	Al Klink
Glenn Miller	PIANO
Jim Priddy	Chummy MacGregor
Paul Tanner	GUITAR
Frank D'Annolfo	Bobby Hackett
DRUMS	BASS
Maurice Purtill	Doc Goldberg

DON'T SIT UNDER THE APPLE TREE
Composer: Sam H. Stept. Lyricists:
Charles Tobias, Lew Brown. Arranger:
Jerry Gray. Recorded for Bluebird
February 18, 1942

TRUMPETS	SAXOPHONES
Mickey McMickle	°Tex Beneke
°John Best	°Willie Schwartz
°Billy May	Ernie Caceres
Steve Lipkins	Al Klink
TROMBONES	Skippy Martin
Glenn Miller	PIANO
Jim Priddy	Chummy MacGregor
Paul Tanner	GUITAR
Frank D'Annolfo	Bobby Hackett
BASS	VOCAL
Doc Goldberg	Marion Hutton,
DRUMS	°Tex Beneke and
Maurice Purtill	The Modernaires

WARM VALLEY
Composer and arranger: Duke Ellington.
Recorded for Victor October 17, 1940

TRUMPETS	PIANO
Wallace Jones	Duke Ellington
Cootie Williams	SAXOPHONES
Rex Stewart	Otto Hardwick
TROMBONES	Johnny Hodges
Joe Nanton	Ben Webster
Juan Tizol	Harry Carney
Lawrence Brown	CLARINET
BASS	Barney Bigard
Jimmy Blanton	GUITAR
DRUMS	Fred Guy
Sonny Greer	

SWING LOW, SWEET CHARIOT
Traditional. Arranger: Deane Kincaide.
Recorded for Victor February 17, 1941

TROMBONES	SAXOPHONES
Tommy Dorsey	Fred Stulce

Les Jenkins	Johnny Mince
George Arus	Paul Mason
Lowell Martin	Heinie Beau
TRUMPETS	Don Lodice
Ziggy Elman	PIANO
Jimmy Blake	Joe Bushkin
Ray Linn	GUITAR
Chuck Peterson	Clark Yocum
DRUMS	BASS
Buddy Rich	Sid Weiss

FLYING HOME
Composers: Benny Goodman, Lionel
Hampton. Arranger: Lionel Hampton.
Recorded for Decca May 26, 1942

TRUMPETS	SAXOPHONES
Ernie Royal	Bob Barefield
Jack Trainer	Ray Perry
Eddie Hutchinson	Illinois Jacquet
°Manny Klein	Jack McVea
TROMBONES	CLARINET
Fred Beckett	Marshall Royal
Sonny Craven	PIANO
Henry Sloan	Milt Buckner
BASS	GUITAR
Vernon Alley	Irving Ashby
DRUMS	VIBRAPHONE
Lee Young	Lionel Hampton

JERSEY BOUNCE
Composers: Bobby Plater, Tiny Bradshaw,
Edward Johnson. Arranger: Mel Powell.
Recorded for Okeh January 15, 1942

TRUMPETS	CLARINET
Jimmie Maxwell	Benny Goodman
Al Davis	SAXOPHONES
Bernie Privin	Clint Neagley
TROMBONES	Sol Kane
Lou McGarity	Vido Musso
Cutty Cutshall	George Berg
PIANO	°Chuck Gentry
Mel Powell	GUITAR
DRUMS	Tom Morgan
Ralph Collier	BASS
	Sid Weiss

I CRIED FOR YOU
Composers: Gus Arnheim and Abe Lyman.
Lyricist: Arthur Freed. Arranger: LeRoy
Holmes. Recorded for Columbia
June 5, 1942

TRUMPETS	SAXOPHONES
Harry James	Claude Lakey
Claude Bowen	George Davis

Nick Buono	Sam Marowitz
Alex Cuozzo	Corky Corcoran
TROMBONES	VIOLINS
Dalton Rizzotto	Leo Zorn
Hoyt Bohannon	Samuel Caplan
Harry Rodgers	John de Voogdt
FRENCH HORN	VIOLA
Willard Culley	William Spear
PIANO	CELLO
Al Lerner	Al Friede
GUITAR	BASS
Ben Heller	Thurman Teague
DRUMS	VOCAL
Mickey Scrima	°Helen Forrest

BASIE BOOGIE
Composers: Count Basie and Milt Ebbins.
"Head" Arrangement. Recorded for Okeh
July 2, 1941

TRUMPETS	PIANO
Edward Lewis	Count Basie
Al Killian	SAXOPHONES
Buck Clayton	Earle Warren
Harry Edison	Jack Washington
TROMBONES	Tab Smith
Robert Scott	Don Byas
Eli Robinson	Buddy Tate
Edward Cuffee	GUITAR
BASS	Freddie Green
Walter Page	
DRUMS	
Jo Jones	

CHARLESTON ALLEY
Composer and arranger: Horace Henderson.
Recorded for Bluebird January 7-23, 1941

TRUMPETS	SAXOPHONES
Lyman Vunk	Charlie Barnet
Bernie Privin	Kurt Bloom
Bobby Burnet	Jimmy Lamare
George Esposito	Leo White
TROMBONES	Conn Humphreys
Don Ruppersberg	PIANO
Bill Robertson	Bill Miller
Spud Murphy	GUITAR
Ford Leary	Bus Etri
DRUMS	BASS
Cliff Leeman	Phil Stephens

AIR MAIL SPECIAL
Composers: Charlie Christian and Benny
Goodman. "Head" arrangement. Recorded
for Columbia March 13, 1941

CLARINET	PIANO
Benny Goodman	Johnny Guarnieri
TRUMPET	GUITAR
Cootie Williams	Charlie Christian
TENOR SAX	BASS
Georgie Auld	Artie Bernstein
DRUMS	
Dave Tough	

°Took part in one or more of the re-creations in this volume.

9:20 SPECIAL
Composer: Earl Warren. Arranger: Buster Harding. Recorded for Okeh April 10, 1941

TRUMPETS	PIANO
Edward Lewis	Count Basie
Al Killian	SAXOPHONES
Buck Clayton	Earle Warren
Harry Edison	Jack Washington
TROMBONES	Tab Smith
Dicky Wells	Don Byas
Dan Minor	Buddy Tate
Edward Cuffee	Coleman Hawkins
DRUMS	GUITAR
Jo Jones	Freddie Greene
	BASS
	Walter Page

THE MAN I LOVE
Composer: George Gershwin. Lyricist: Ira Gershwin. Arranger: Ed Sauter. Recorded for Columbia November 13, 1940

TRUMPETS	CLARINET
Alec Fila	Benny Goodman
Jimmie Maxwell	SAXOPHONES
Irving Goodman	Skippy Martin
TROMBONES	Gus Bivona
Lou McGarity	Bob Snyder
Red Gingler	Georgie Auld
BASS	Jack Henderson
Artie Bernstein	PIANO
DRUMS	Bernie Leighton
Harry Jaeger	GUITAR
	Mike Bryan
	VOCAL
	°Helen Forrest

SUMMIT RIDGE DRIVE
Composer and arranger: Artie Shaw. Recorded for Victor September 3, 1940

CLARINET	TRUMPET
Artie Shaw	Billy Butterfield
BASS	HARPSICHORD
Jud DeNaut	Johnny Guarnieri
DRUMS	GUITAR
°Nick Fatool	°Al Hendrickson

ADIOS
Composer: Enric Madriguera. Arranger: Jerry Gray. Recorded for Bluebird June 25, 1941

TRUMPETS	SAXOPHONES
Mickey McMickle	Hal McIntyre
°John Best	°Tex Beneke
°Billy May	°Willie Schwartz
Ray Anthony	Ernie Caceres
TROMBONES	Al Klink
Glenn Miller	PIANO
Jim Priddy	Chummy MacGregor
Paul Tanner	GUITAR
Warren Smith	Bill Conway
DRUMS	BASS
Maurice Purtill	Doc Goldberg

GOLDEN WEDDING
Composer: Gabriel-Marie. Arranger: Jiggs Noble. Recorded for Decca September 27, 1940

TRUMPETS	CLARINET
Bob Price	Woody Herman
Steady Nelson	SAXOPHONES
Cappy Lewis	Herb Tompkins
TROMBONES	Bill Vitale
Bud Smith	Saxie Mansfield
Neal Reid	Mickey Folus
BASS	PIANO
Walt Yoder	Tommy Linehan
DRUMS	GUITAR
Frank Carlson	Hy White

BEYOND THE BLUE HORIZON
Composers: Richard A. Whiting and W. Franke Harling. Arranger: Artie Shaw. Recorded for Victor September 3, 1941

TRUMPET	CLARINET
Lee Castaldo	Artie Shaw
TROMBONE	SAXOPHONE
Ray Conniff	Georgie Auld
BASS	PIANO
Eddie McKimmey	Johnny Guarnieri
DRUMS	GUITAR
Dave Tough	Mike Bryan
	STRINGS 15

CHATTANOOGA CHOO CHOO
Composer: Harry Warren. Lyricist: Mack Gordon. Arranger: Jerry Gray. Recorded for Bluebird May 7, 1941

TRUMPETS	SAXOPHONES
Mickey McMickle	Hal McIntyre
°John Best	°Tex Beneke
°Billy May	°Willie Schwartz
Ray Anthony	Ernie Caceres
TROMBONES	Al Klink
Glenn Miller	PIANO
Jim Priddy	Chummy MacGregor
Paul Tanner	GUITAR
Frank D'Annolfo	Jack Lathrop
BASS	VOCAL
Trigger Alpert	°Tex Beneke and The
DRUMS	Modernaires
Maurice Purtill	

AUTUMN NOCTURNE
Composer: Josef Myrow. Arranger: Claude Thornhill. Recorded for Columbia October 6, 1941

TRUMPETS	PIANO
°Conrad Gozzo	Claude Thornhill
Rusty Dedrick	SAXOPHONES
Bob Sprental	Dale Brown
TROMBONES	Jack Ferrier
Tasso Harris	Lester Merkin
Bob Jenney	John Nelson
GUITAR	Hammond Russum
Barry Galbraith	CLARINETS
BASS	Irving Fazola
Harvey Cell	Jimmy Abato
DRUMS	FRENCH HORNS
°Nick Fatool	Richard Hall
	Vince Jacobs

BENNY RIDES AGAIN
Composer and arranger: Eddie Sauter. Recorded for Columbia November 13, 1940

TRUMPETS	CLARINET
Alec Fila	Benny Goodman
Jimmie Maxwell	SAXOPHONES
Cootie Williams	Skippy Martin
Irving Goodman	Gus Bivona
TROMBONES	Bob Snyder
Lou McGarity	Georgie Auld
Red Gingler	Jack Henderson
BASS	PIANO
Artie Bernstein	Bernie Leighton
DRUMS	GUITAR
Harry Jaeger	Mike Bryan

THE MOLE
Composers: LeRoy Holmes and Harry James. Arranger: LeRoy Holmes. Recorded for Columbia December 30, 1941

TRUMPETS	SAXOPHONES
Harry James	Claude Lakey
Claude Bowen	Sam Marowitz
Nick Buono	Dave Matthews
TROMBONES	Clint Davis
Dalton Rizzotto	VIOLINS
Hoyt Bohannon	Alex Pevsner
Harry Rodgers	Sindel Kopp
GUITAR	Leo Zorn
Ben Heller	VIOLA
BASS	Bill Spears
Thurman Teague	CELLO
DRUMS	Al Fried
Mickey Scrima	PIANO
	Al Lerner

A SMO-O-O-TH ONE
Composer: Benny Goodman. "Head" arrangement. Recorded for Columbia March 13, 1941

CLARINET	TENOR SAXOPHONE
Benny Goodman	Georgie Auld
TRUMPET	PIANO
Cootie Williams	Johnny Guarnieri
BASS	GUITAR
Artie Bernstein	Charlie Christian
DRUMS	
Dave Tough	

BLUE FLAME
Composers and arrangers: Jiggs Noble and Joe Bishop. Recorded for Decca February 13, 1941

TRUMPETS	CLARINET
Johnny Owens	Woody Herman
Cappy Lewis	SAXOPHONES
Steady Nelson	Herb Tompkins
TROMBONES	Eddie Scalzi
Neal Reid	Saxie Mansfield
Bud Smith	Mickey Folus
Vic Hamann	PIANO
DRUMS	Tommy Linehan
Frank Carlson	GUITAR
	Hy White
	BASS
	Walt Yoder

WELL, GIT IT!
Composer and arranger: Sy Oliver. Recorded for Victor March 9-13, 1942

TRUMPETS	SAXOPHONES
Ziggy Elman	Manny Gershman
Jimmy Blake	Bruce Snyder
Chuck Peterson	Fred Stulce
°Manny Klein	Heinie Beau
TROMBONES	Don Lodice
Tommy Dorsey	PIANO
Dave Jacobs	Milt Raskin
George Arus	GUITAR
Jimmy Skiles	Clark Yocum
DRUMS	BASS
Buddy Rich	Phil Stevens

PERDIDO
Composer: Juan Tizol. Arranger: Duke Ellington. Recorded for Victor January 21, 1942

TRUMPETS	PIANO
Wallace Jones	Duke Ellington
Ray Nance	SAXOPHONES
Rex Stewart	Otto Hardwick
TROMBONES	Johnny Hodges
Joe Nanton	Ben Webster
Juan Tizol	Harry Carney
Lawrence Brown	CLARINET
BASS	Barney Bigard
Junior Raglin	GUITAR
DRUMS	Fred Guy
Sonny Greer	

SONG OF THE VOLGA BOATMEN

Traditional. Arranger: Bill Finegan.
Recorded for Bluebird January 17, 1941

TRUMPETS	SAXOPHONES
Mickey McMickle	Hal McIntyre
*John Best	*Tex Beneke
*Billy May	*Willie Schwartz
Ray Anthony	Ernie Caceres
TROMBONES	Al Klink
Glenn Miller	PIANO
Jim Priddy	Chummy MacGregor
Paul Tanner	GUITAR
Frank D'Annolfo	Jack Lathrop
DRUMS	BASS
Maurice Purtill	Trigger Alpert

CONTRASTS

Composer: Jimmy Dorsey. Arranger: Fred Slack. Recorded for Decca April 3, 1940

TRUMPETS	SAXOPHONES
Johnny Napton	Jimmy Dorsey
Nate Kazebier	Milt Yaner
Shorty Solomson	Sam Rubinwitch
	Charles Frazier
	Herbie Haymer

TROMBONES	PIANO
Jerry Rosa	Joe Lipman
Sonny Lee	GUITAR
Don Mattison	Guy Smith
DRUMS	BASS
Buddy Schutz	Jack Ryan

STRICTLY INSTRUMENTAL

Composers: Edgar William Battle, Bennie Benjamin, Sol Marcus and Edward Seiler. Arranger: Jack Matthias. Recorded for Columbia December 30, 1941

TRUMPETS	SAXOPHONES
Harry James	Claude Lakey
Claude Bowen	Sam Marowitz
Nick Buono	Dave Matthews
TROMBONES	Clint Davis
Dalton Rizzotto	PIANO
Hoyt Bohannon	Al Lerner
Harry Rodgers	GUITAR
DRUMS	Ben Heller
Mickey Scrima	BASS
	Thurman Teague

DANCING IN THE DARK

Composer: Arthur Schwartz. Arranger: Lenny Hayton. Recorded for Victor January 23, 1941

TRUMPETS	CLARINET
George Wendt	Artie Shaw
Jimmy Cathcart	SAXOPHONES
Billy Butterfield	Les Robinson
TROMBONES	Neely Plumb
Jack Jenney	Bus Bassey
Vernon Brown	Jerry Jerome
Ray Conniff	PIANO
BASS	Johnny Guarnieri
Jud DeNaut	GUITAR
DRUMS	*Al Hendrickson
*Nick Fatool	STRINGS 9

AMERICAN PATROL

Composer: Frank W. Meacham. Arranger: Jerry Gray. Recorded for Victor April 2, 1942

TRUMPETS	SAXOPHONES
Mickey McMickle	*Tex Beneke
*John Best	*Willie Schwartz
*Billy May	Ernie Caceres
Steve Lipkins	Al Klink
TROMBONES	Skippy Martin
Glenn Miller	PIANO
Jim Priddy	Chummy MacGregor
Paul Tanner	GUITAR
Frank D'Annolfo	Bobby Hackett
DRUMS	BASS
Maurice Purtill	Doc Goldberg

ACKNOWLEDGMENTS

A number of musicians, bandleaders, arrangers, singers, managers, songwriters and others knowledgeable on swing music helped with source material for this book. The editors wish to thank the following for their assistance: Angelo Badolato, Ray Bauduc, Mrs. Jean Berger, Bob Crosby, June Crosby, Stanley Dance, Thomas F. Dorsey III, Frank Driggs, Bob Eberly, Ray Eberle, Jack Egan, Bob Haggart, John Hammond, Earl Hines, Gene Krupa, Lansing Lamont, Yank Lawson, Johnny Mercer, Alan P. Merriam, Francis O'Keefe, Sy Oliver, Bob Ottum, Larry Parker, Charles Peterson, Mrs. Ella K. Pratt, William S. Randolph, I. M. Rappaport, Gil Rodin, Eddie Sauter, Shorty Sherock, Mrs. Marshall Stearns, Larry Wagner, Helen Ward, Dicky Wells.

Many Time Inc. departments and staff members helped in the preparation of this volume. A few of them are: Anne Drayton and Carmela Lotrecchiano of the office of LIFE's Director of Photography; Marcia Gauger, Nancy Faber and Barbara Wilkins of the Time-Life News Service; Marjorie Chapman of the Time Inc. Picture Collection; George Karas and Herbert Orth of the Photographic Laboratory.

Songs quoted from in this volume are copyrighted as follows: *Mairzy Doats* in 1943 by Miller Music Corporation; *The Hut-Sut Song* in 1941 by Schumann Music Co.; *Three Little Fishes* in 1939 by Santly Joy Select Inc.; *The Flat Foot Floogee* in 1938 by Green Bros. & Knight; and *Dancing in the Dark* in 1931 by Harms Inc.

CREDITS

4, 5—Ralph Crane from Black Star
8—Photo Files
9—Karger-Pix
10—Nina Leen-Pix
11—David Gahr
12 through 15—drawings by Michael Ramus
16—New York Daily News Photo
17—Marie Hansen
18 through 21—Gjon Mili
22—Panama Francis
23—Panama Francis

24, 25—l. Panama Francis; r. t. & b. Nappy Lamare
26, 27—Peter Stackpole
28, 29—t. l. Karger-Pix; t. c. Hart Preston; t.r. Photo Files; b. l!, c. & r. Charles Peterson
30—t. United Press International; b. Wide World Photos
33—Alfred Eisenstaedt
34—l. & r. Down Beat
35—United Press Photo
36—t. & b. Down Beat

37—t. & b. Photo Files
38—Culver Pictures
39—Lou Valentino
40—t. courtesy Thomas F. Dorsey III; c. United Press International; b. George Van
41—t. Los Angeles Examiner Photo from International; b. Down Beat
42—courtesy Billboard Magazine
43—Down Beat
44, 45—Nappy Lamare
46—Down Beat

47—Photo Files
48—Mrs. Jean Berger
49—Photo Files
50—t. Time Inc. Picture Collection; c. Milton Washington; b. l. & r. Mrs. Jean Berger
51—t. Bob Crosby; b. Defense Department, Marine Corps
52, 53—Bob Crosby

Abbreviations: b. bottom; c., center; l., left; r., right; t., top